How To Draw Ninja

A Step by Step Guide

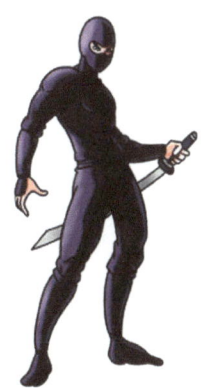

Copyright © 2019 by SketchPert Press

All rights reserved. This book or any portion thereof may not be reproduced or used in any manner whatsoever without the express written permission of the publisher except for the use of brief quotations in a book review.

Printed in the United States of America

9781704542065

INSTRUCTIONS

HERE YOU WILL FIND THE STEPS NECECESSARY TO REPLICATE THE POSES FOUND THROUGHOUT THIS BOOK.

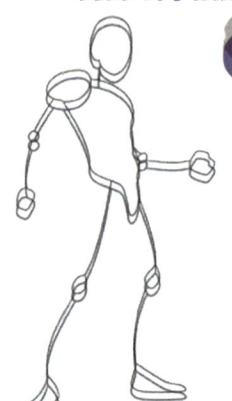

1 EVERY POSE STARTS OUT WITH A BASIC OUTLINE OF THE POSE. THIS IS DONE BY SKETCHING OUT A SIMPLE STICK FIGURE FOR THE BODY. FOR THE BEST RESULTS TRY USING CIRCLES FOR THE JOINTS, SHOULDERS AND HANDS.

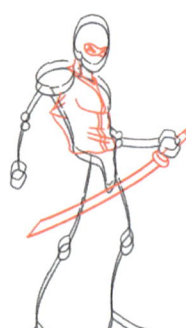

2 NEXT WE WILL BEGIN FLESHING OUT THE FIGURE. START WITH THE AREAS OUTLINED IN RED. THEN ADD THE FIGURE'S FINGERS

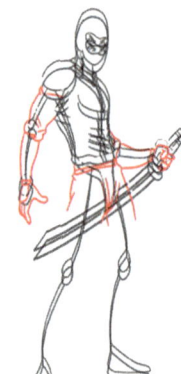

3 IN THE THIRD STEP, CONTINUE TO FLESH OUT THE FIGURE EVEN FURTHER BY FOCUSING ON THE UPPER LIMBS. HERE WE'LL ALSO FURTHER DEFINE THE WEAPONS.

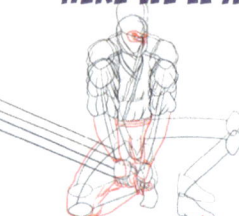

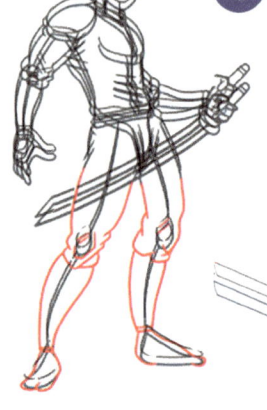

4 NEXT MOVE ON TO THE LOWER HALF OF THE BODY. ONCE YOU HAVE THE FULL BODY SKETCHED OUT, BEGIN ERASING ANY OF THE REMAINING LINES FROM THE ORIGINAL OUTLINES.

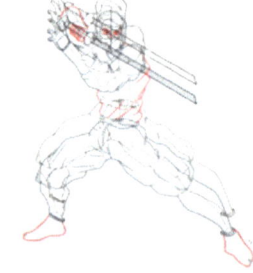
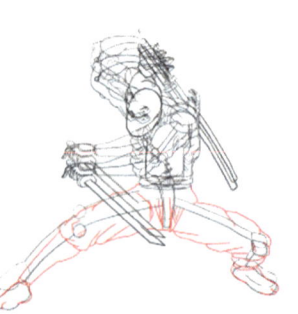

GRAPHING PAPER

Opposite each guide you will find a blank sheet of 4x4 graph paper. By focusing in on the grids you can better pinpoint and emulate the art featured in the guides.

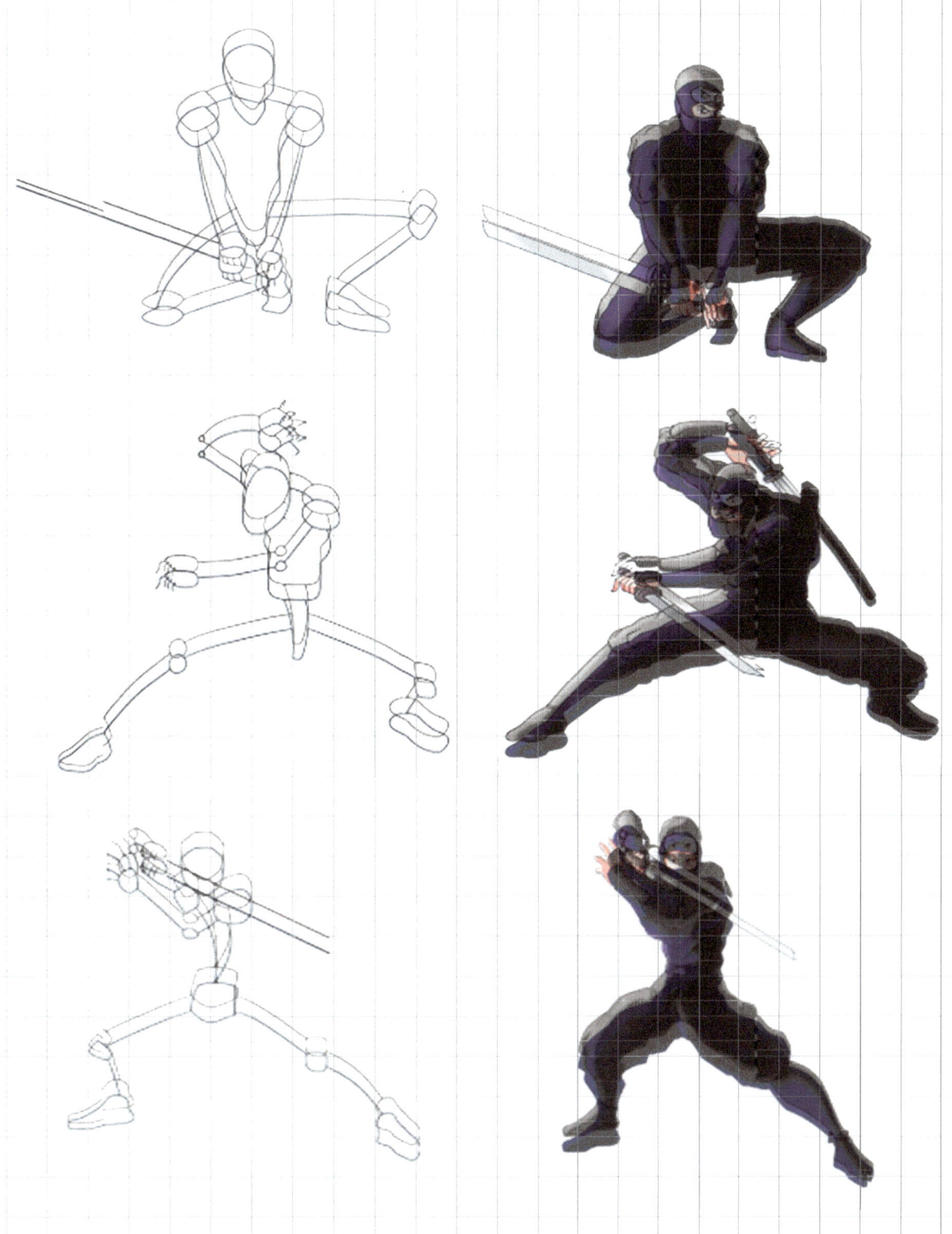

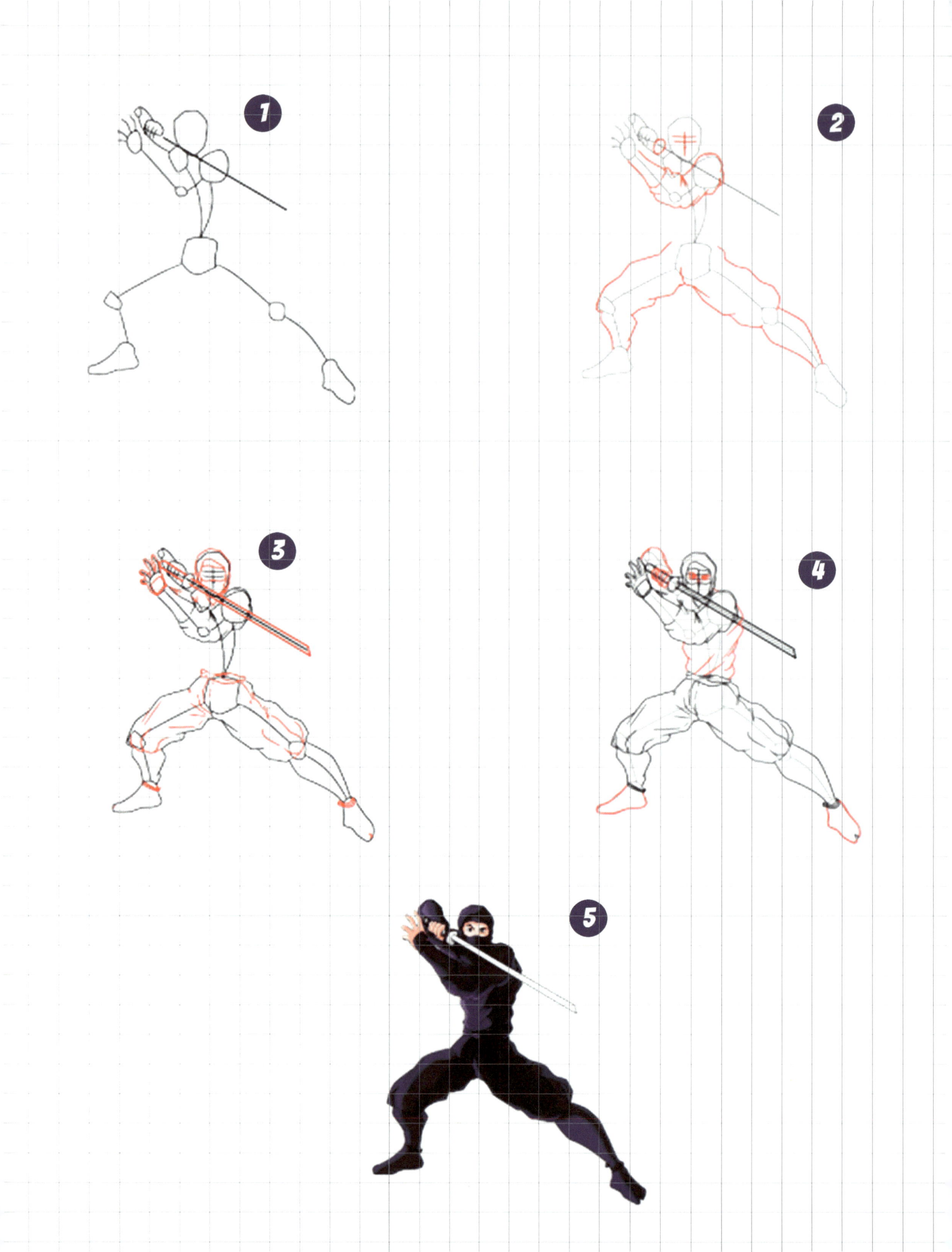

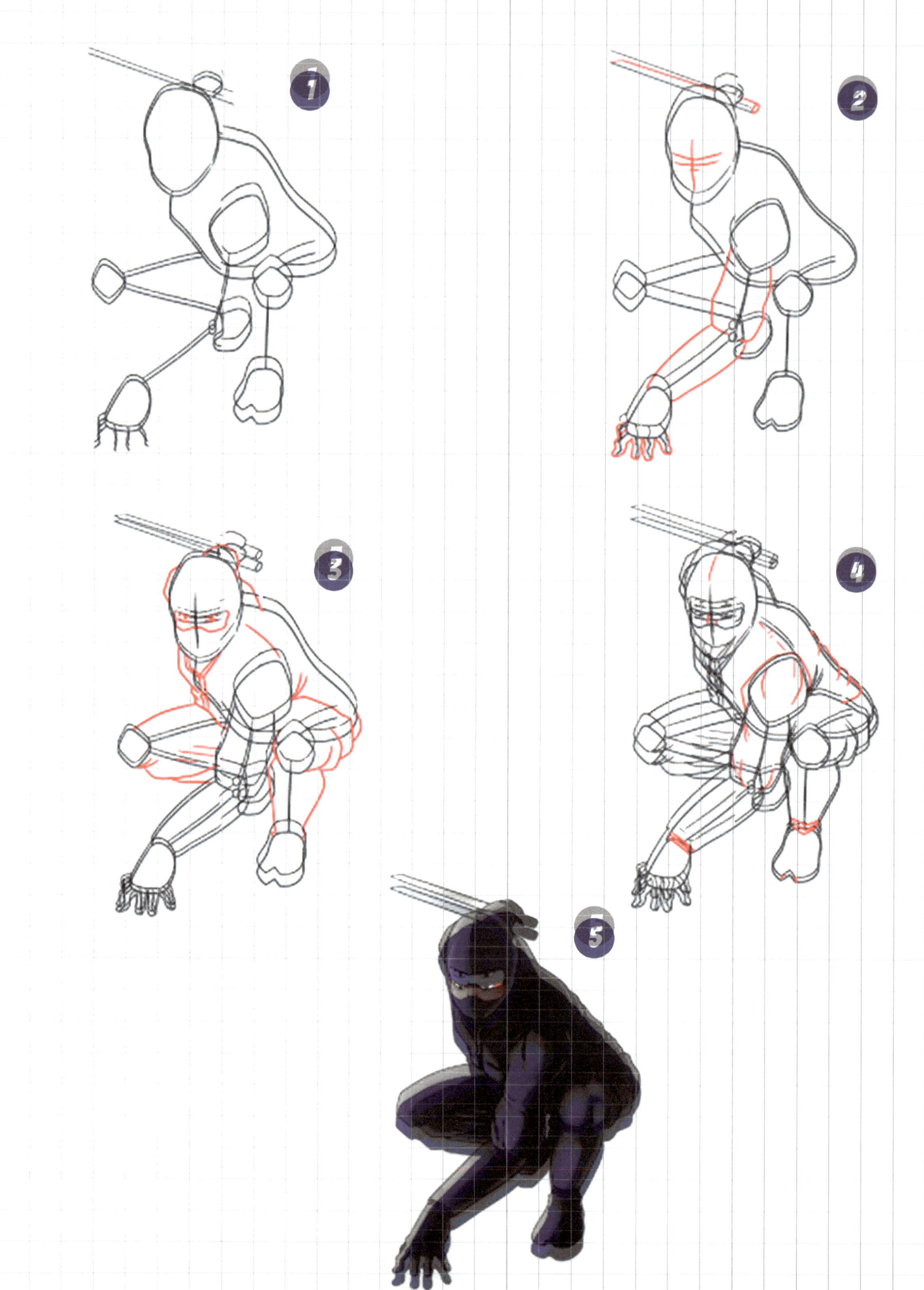

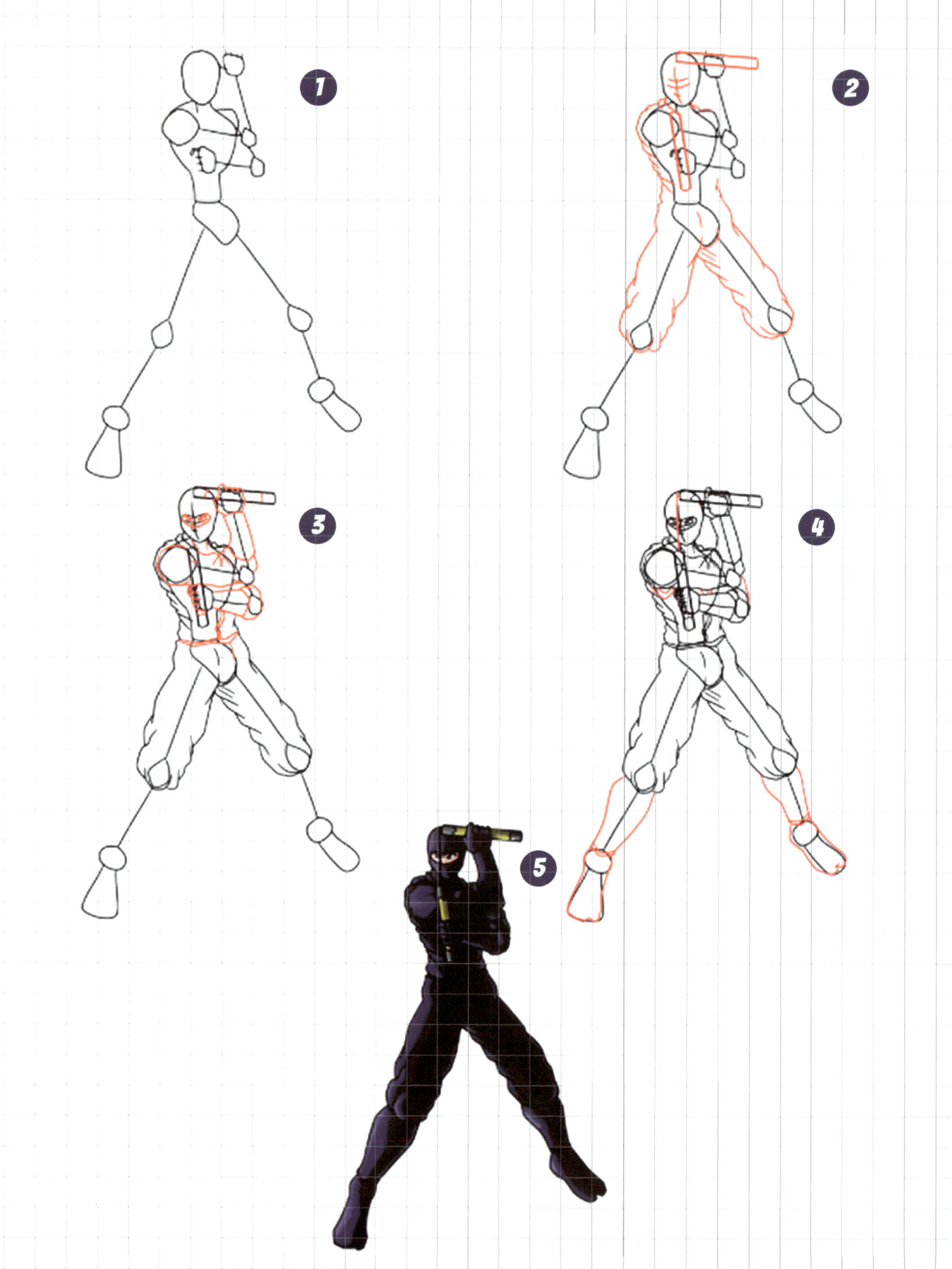

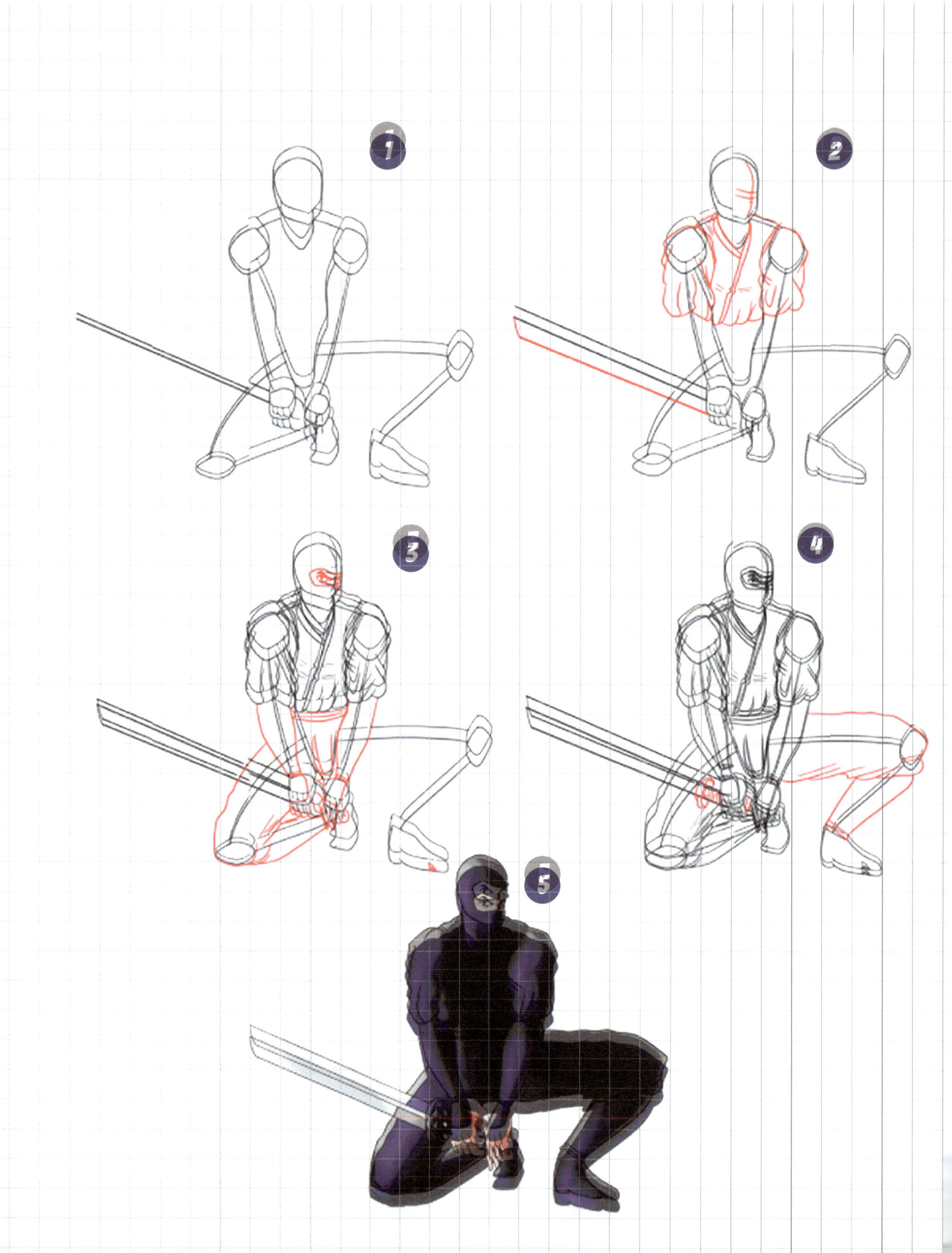

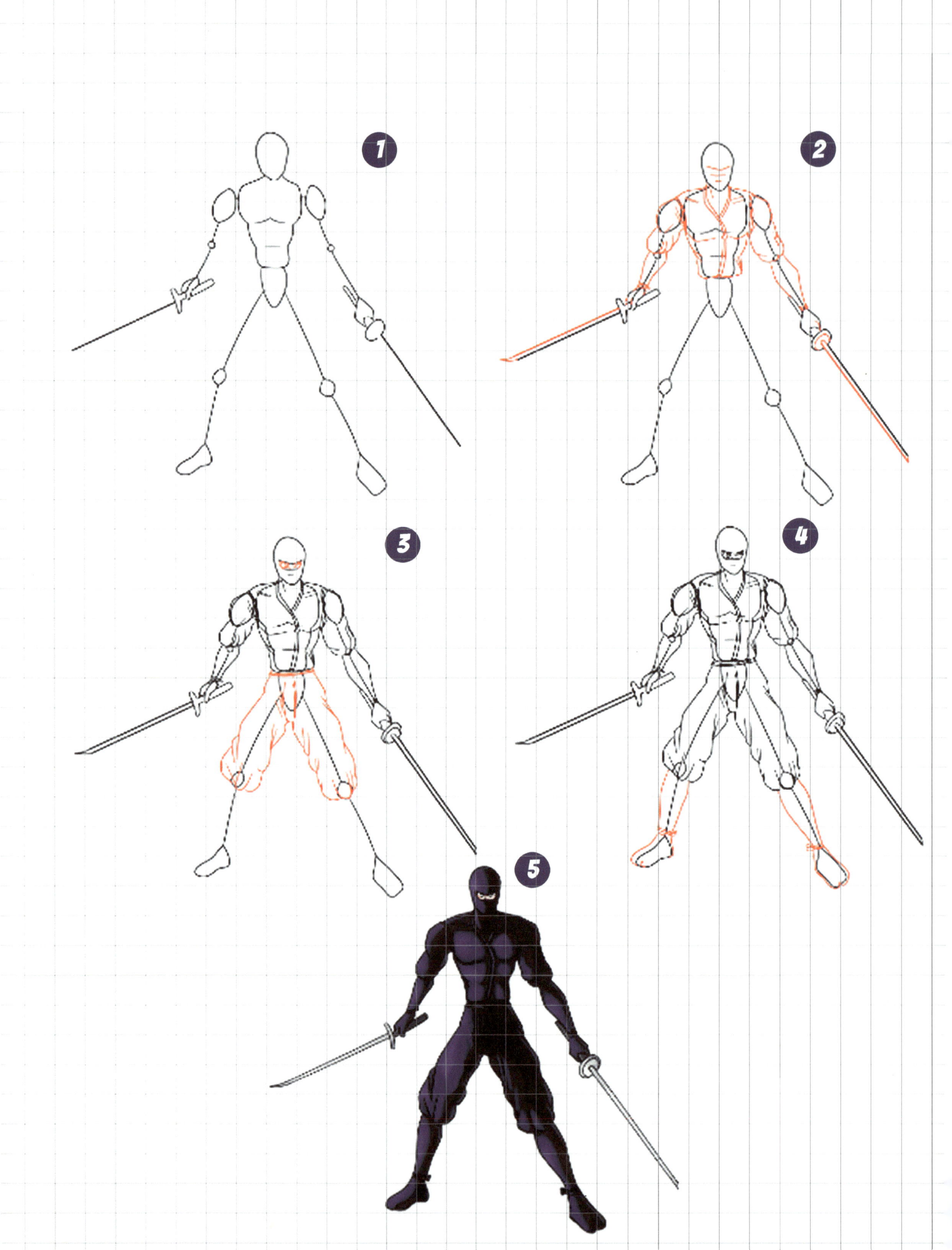

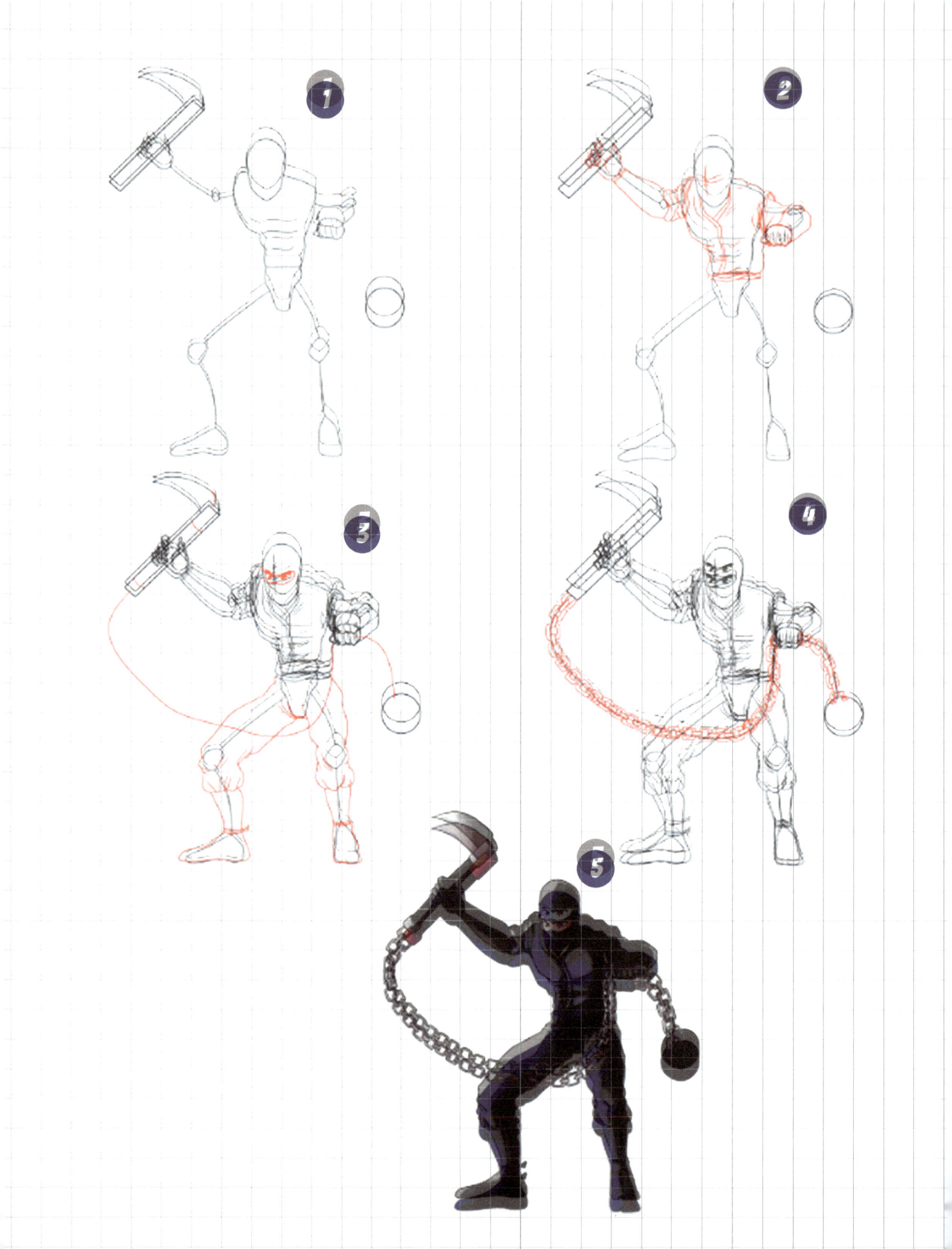

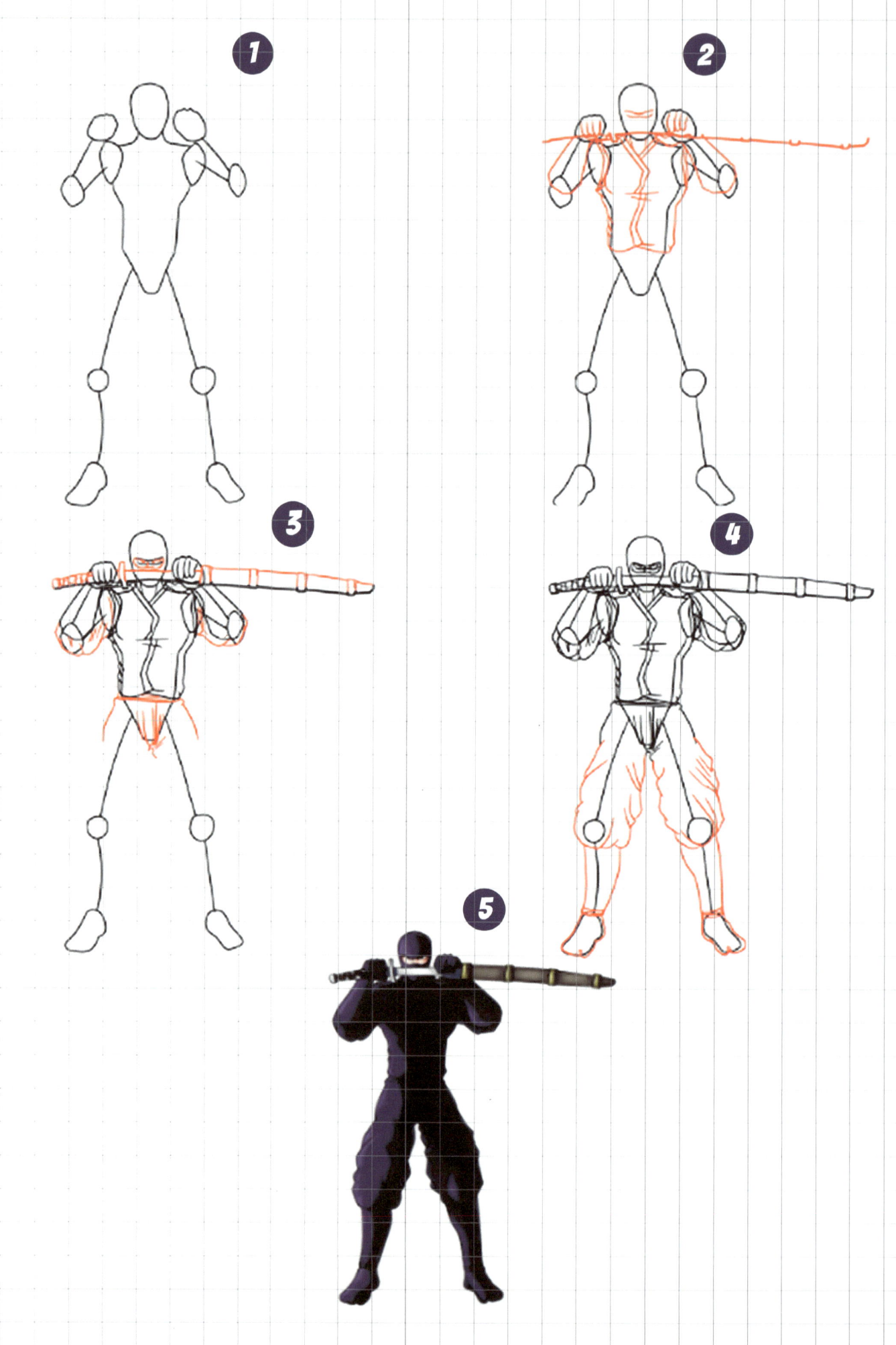

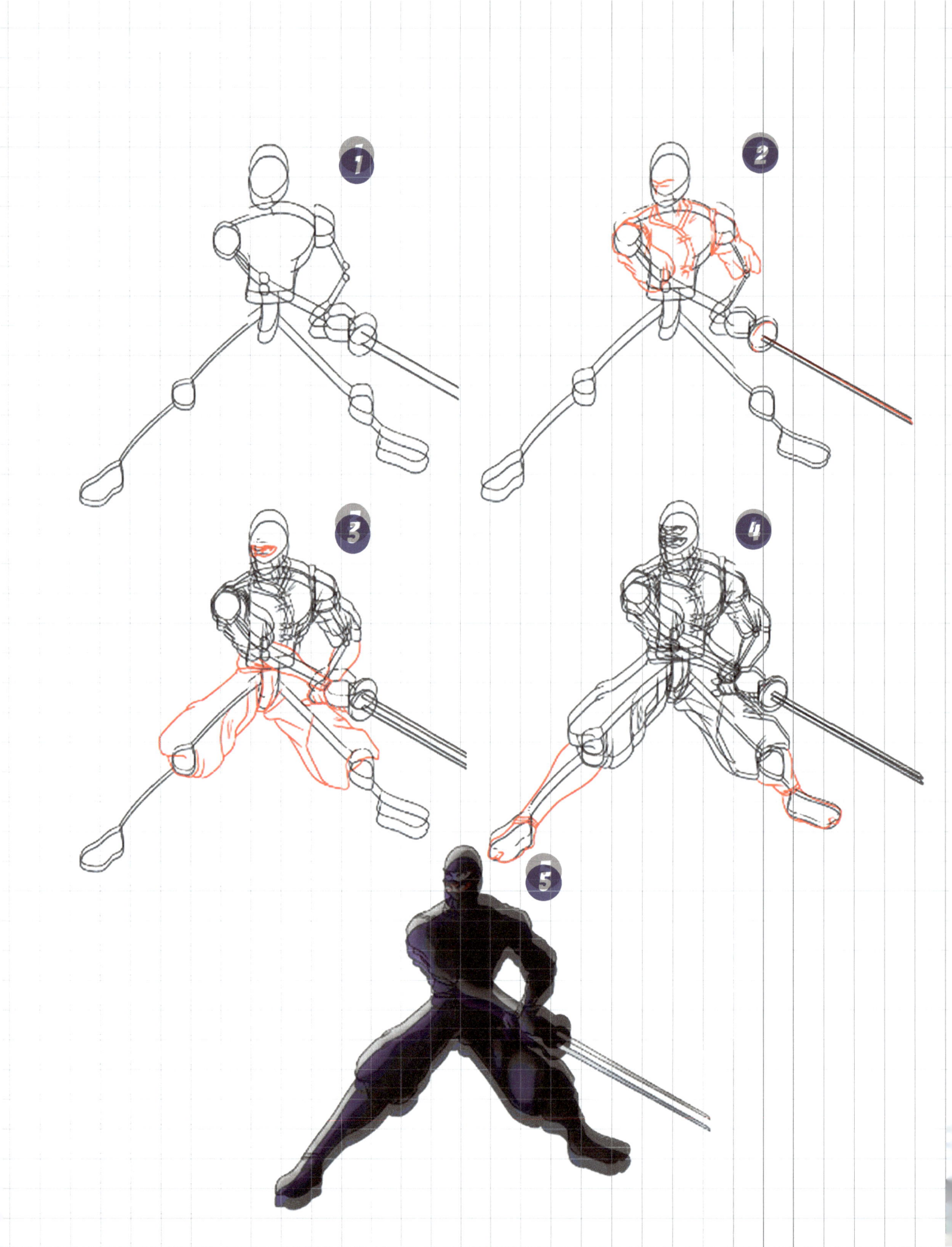

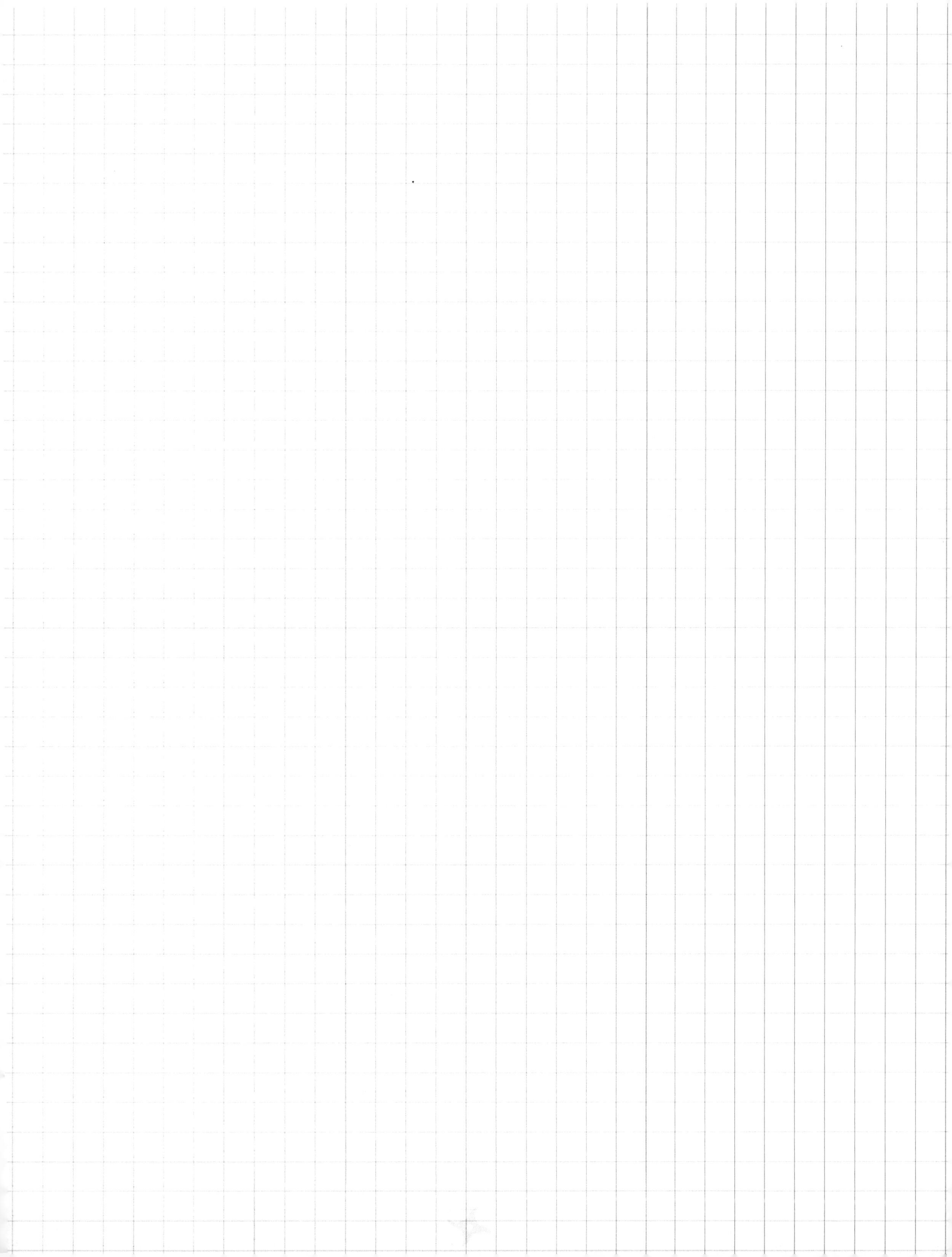

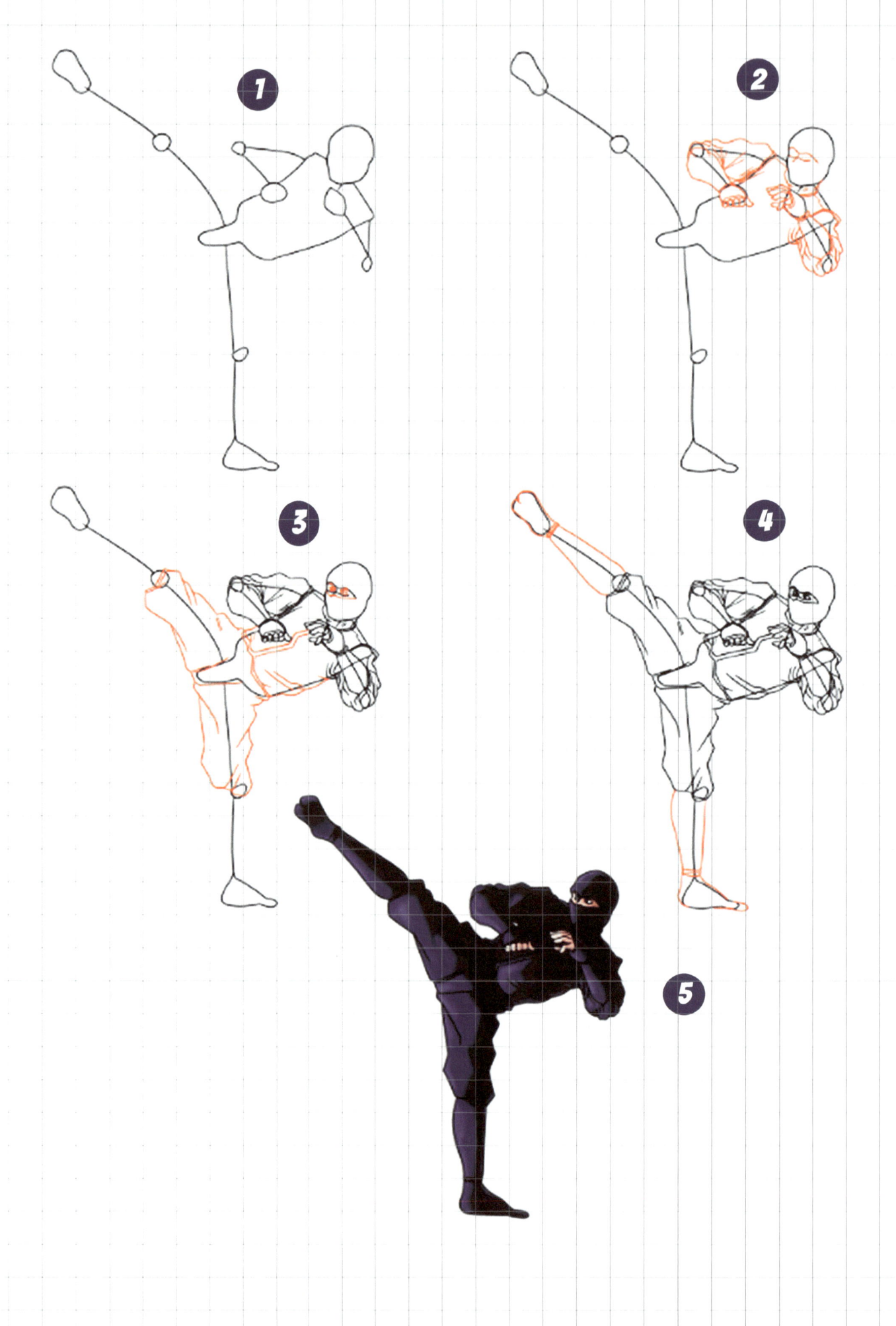

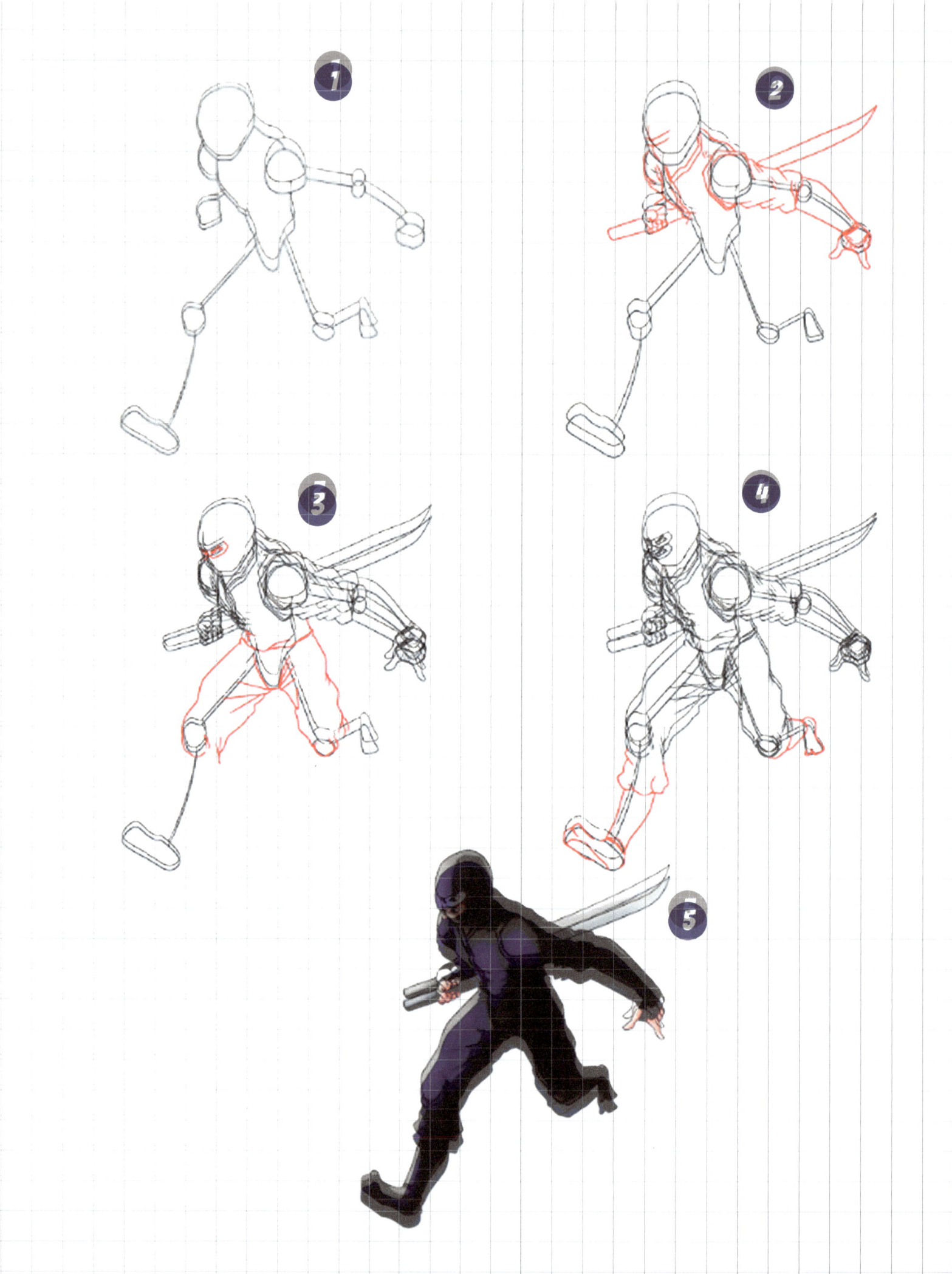

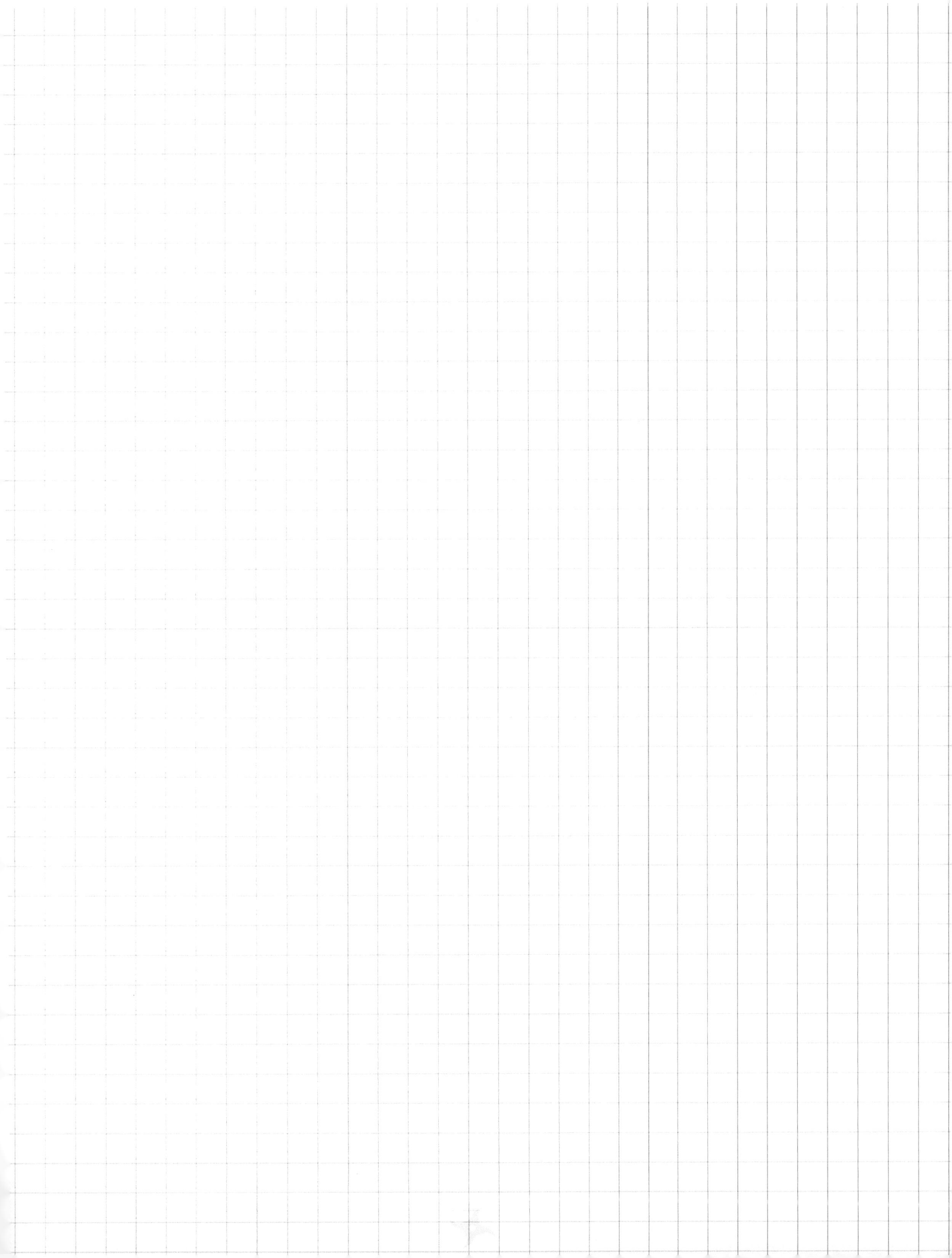

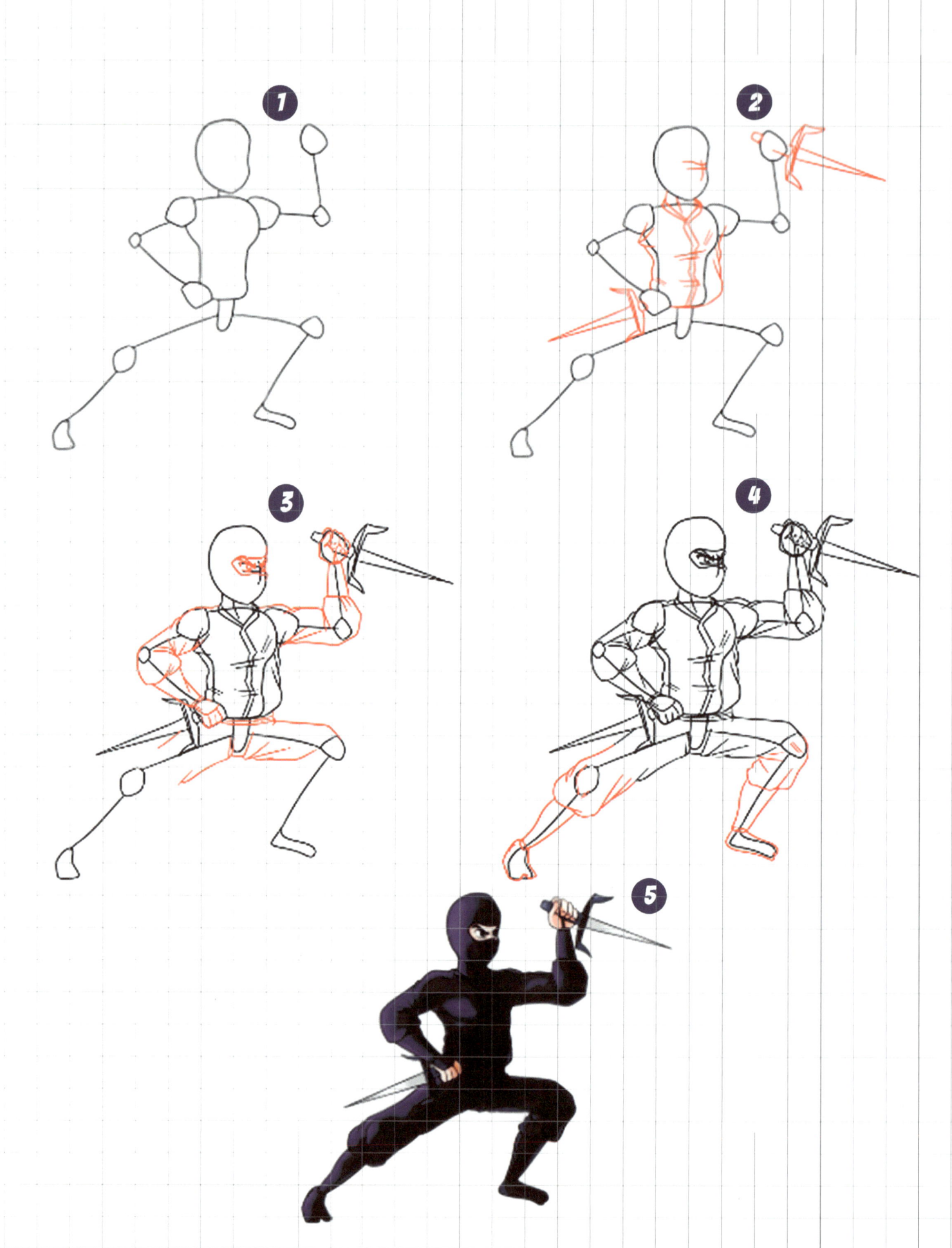

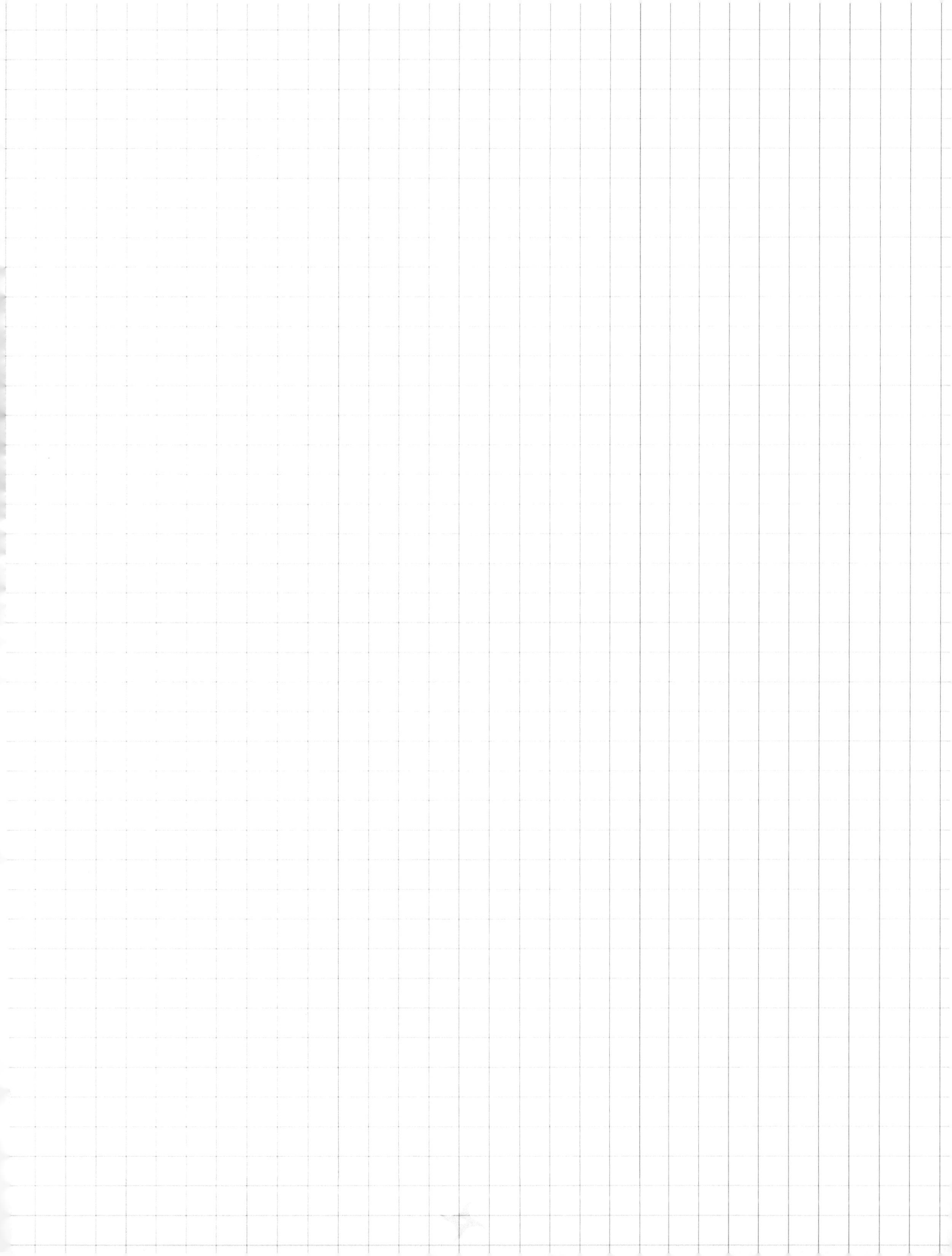

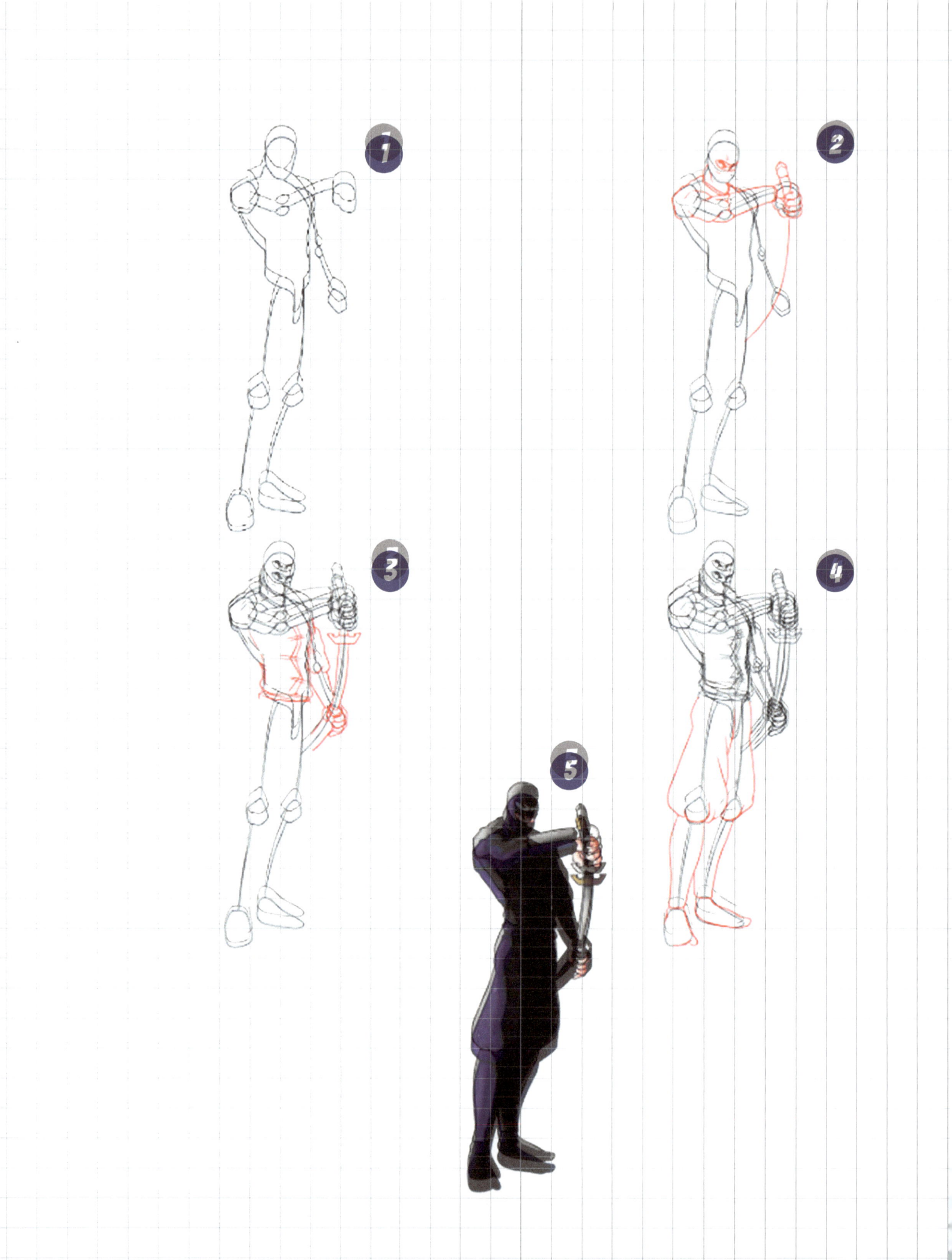

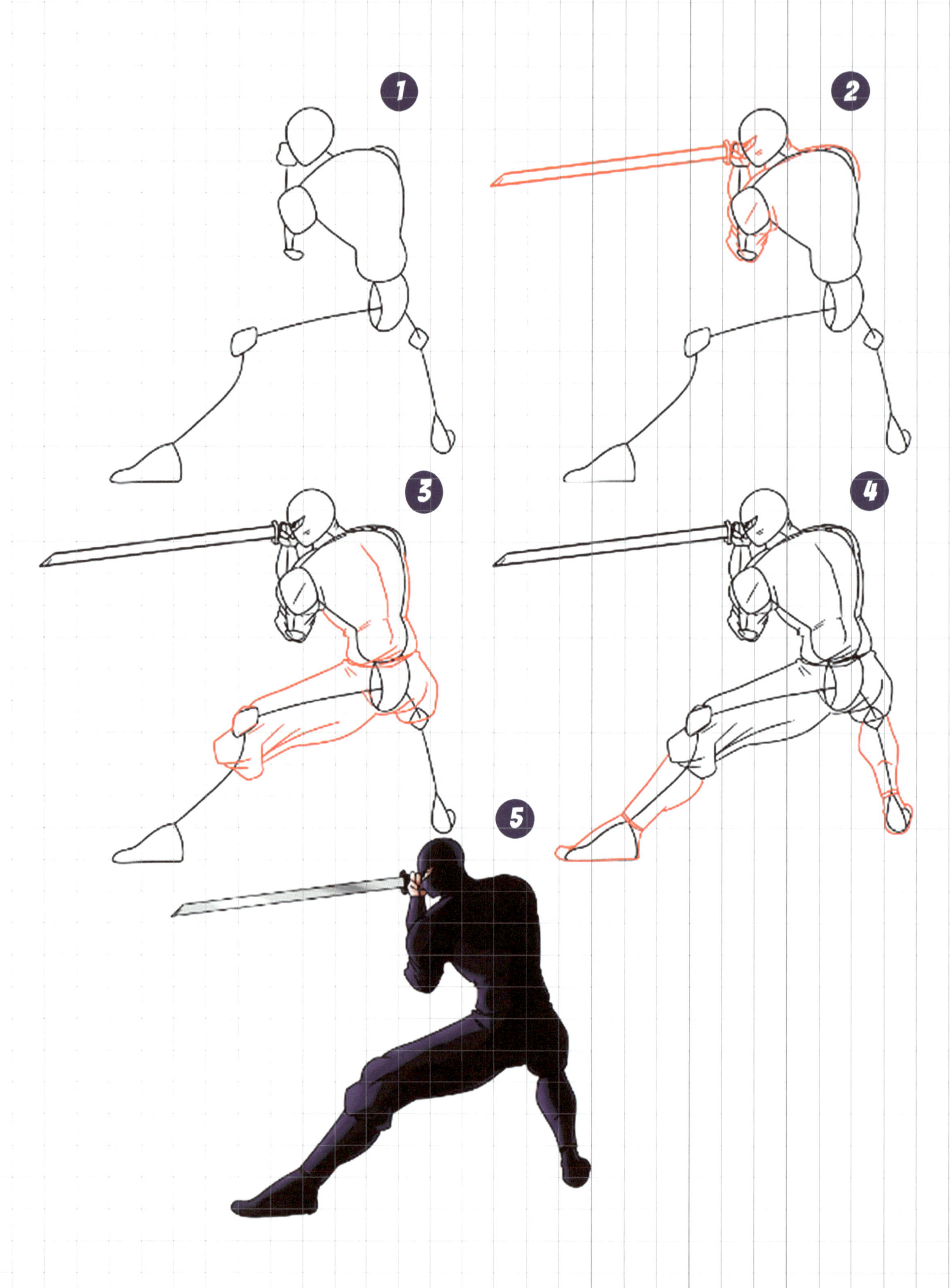

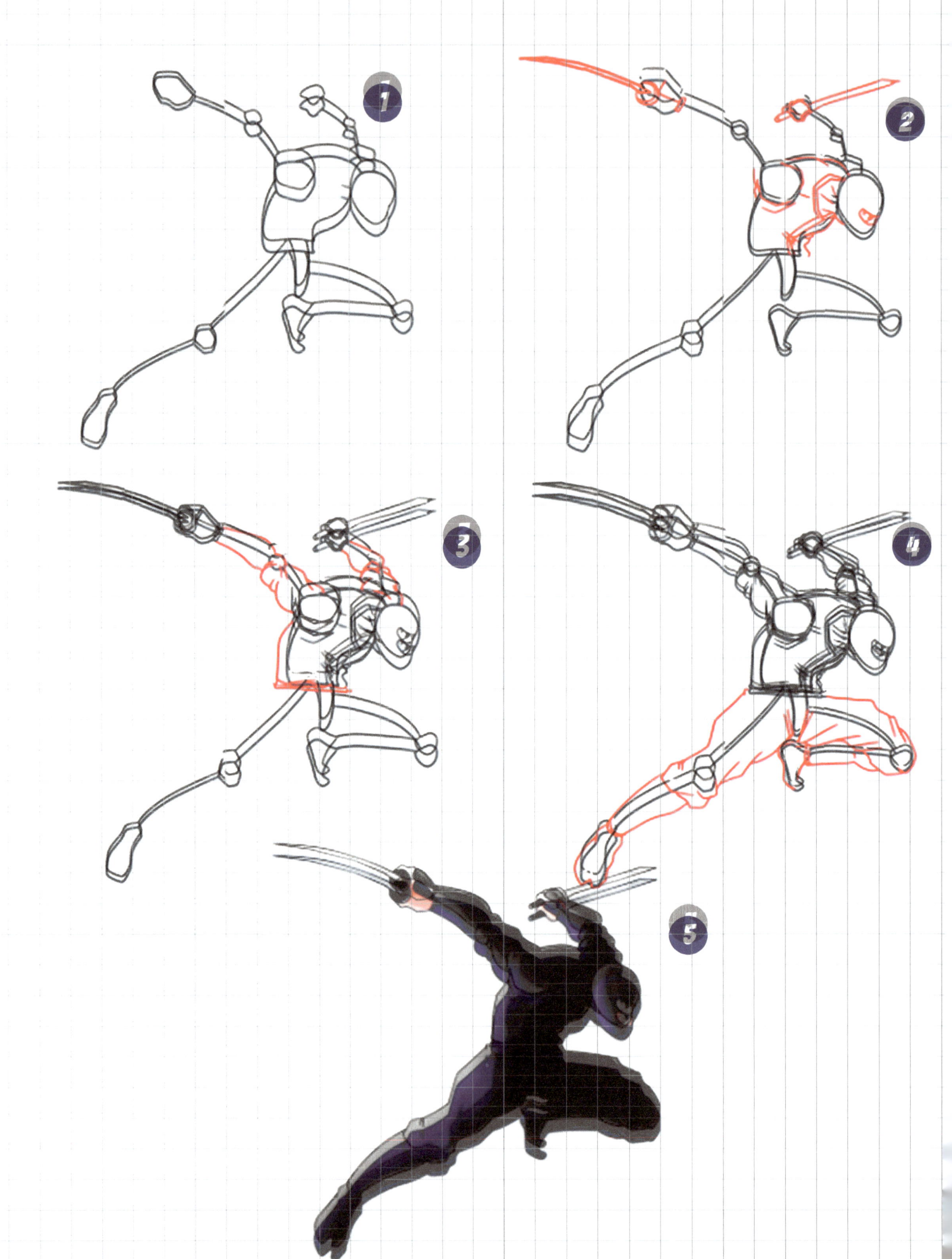

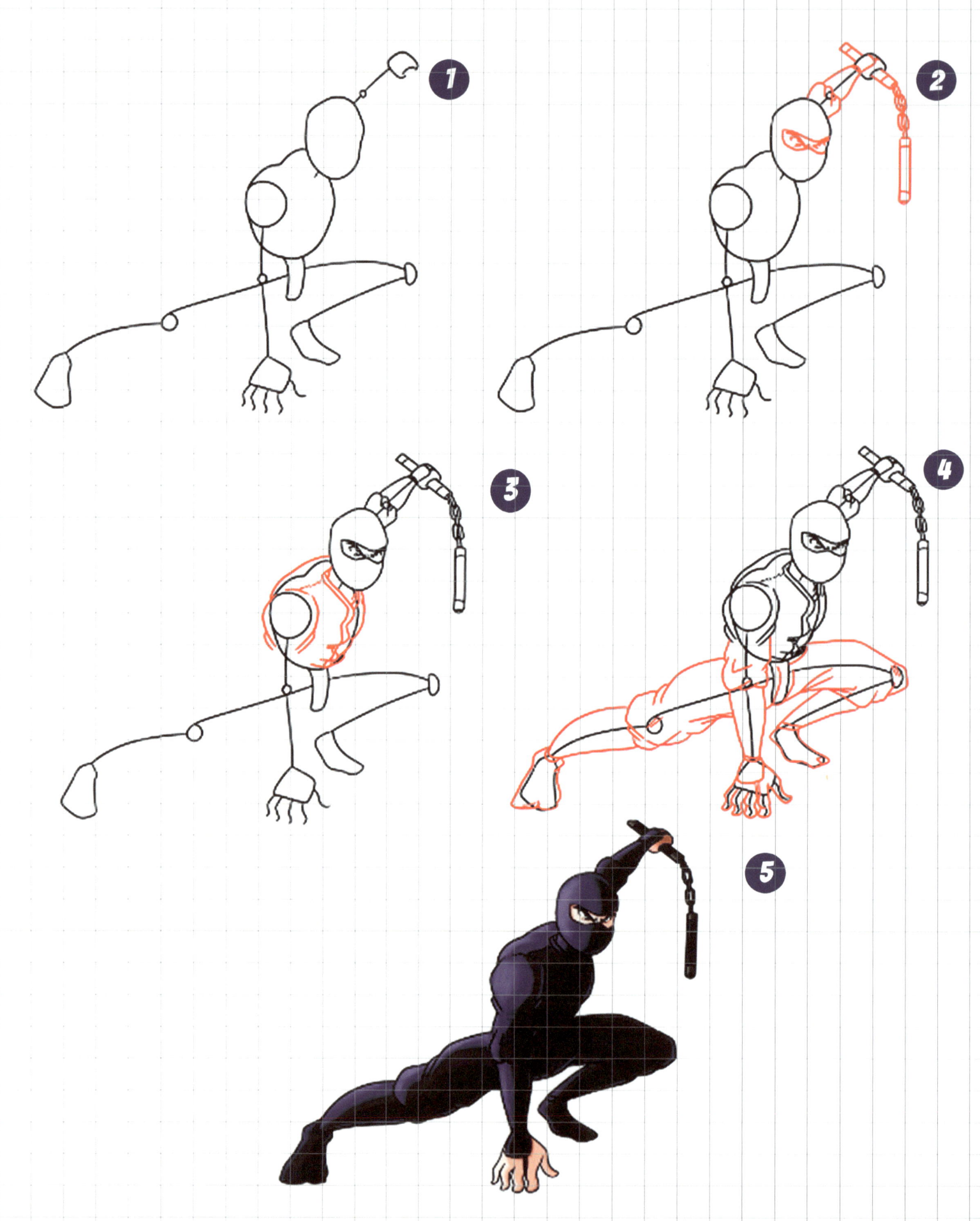

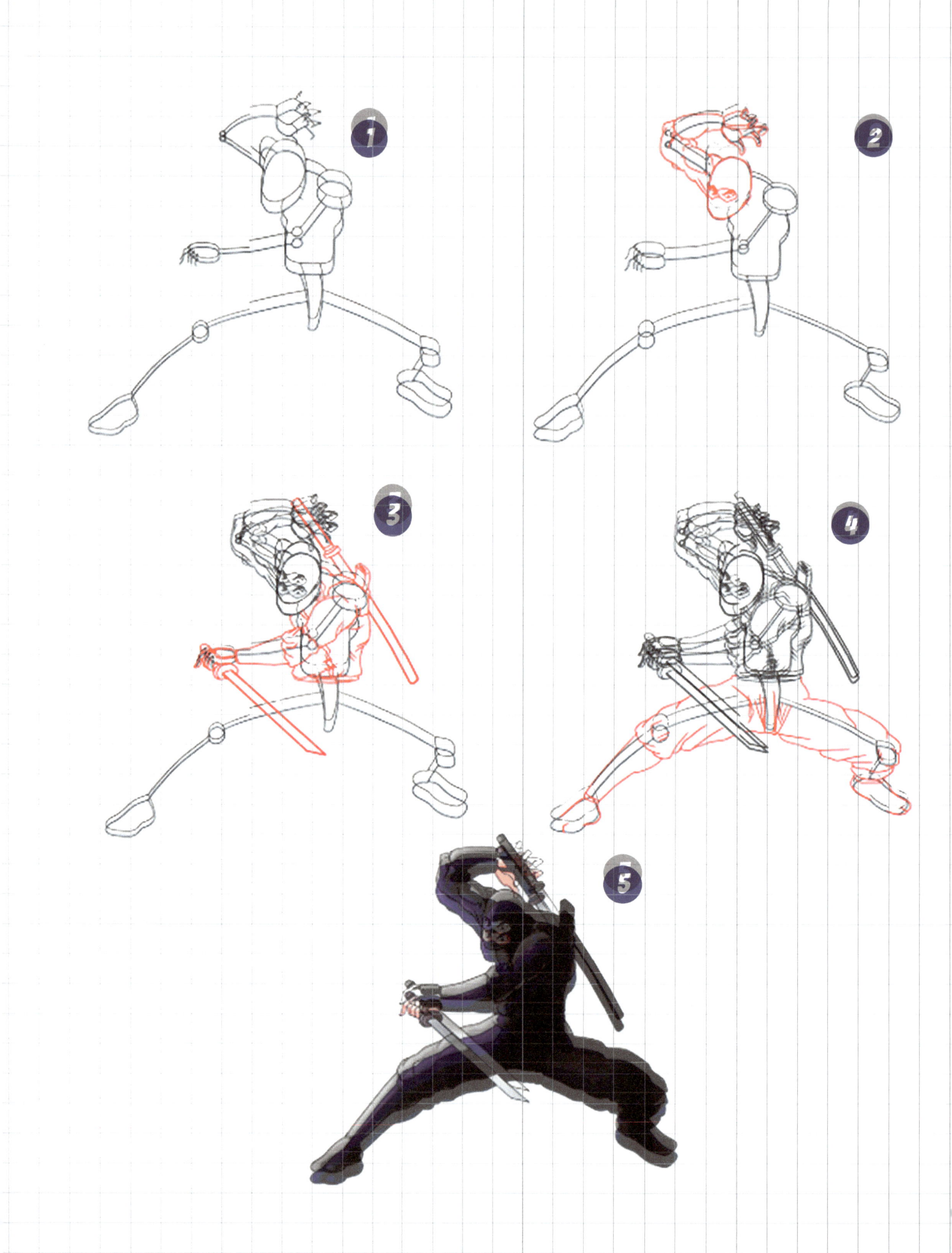

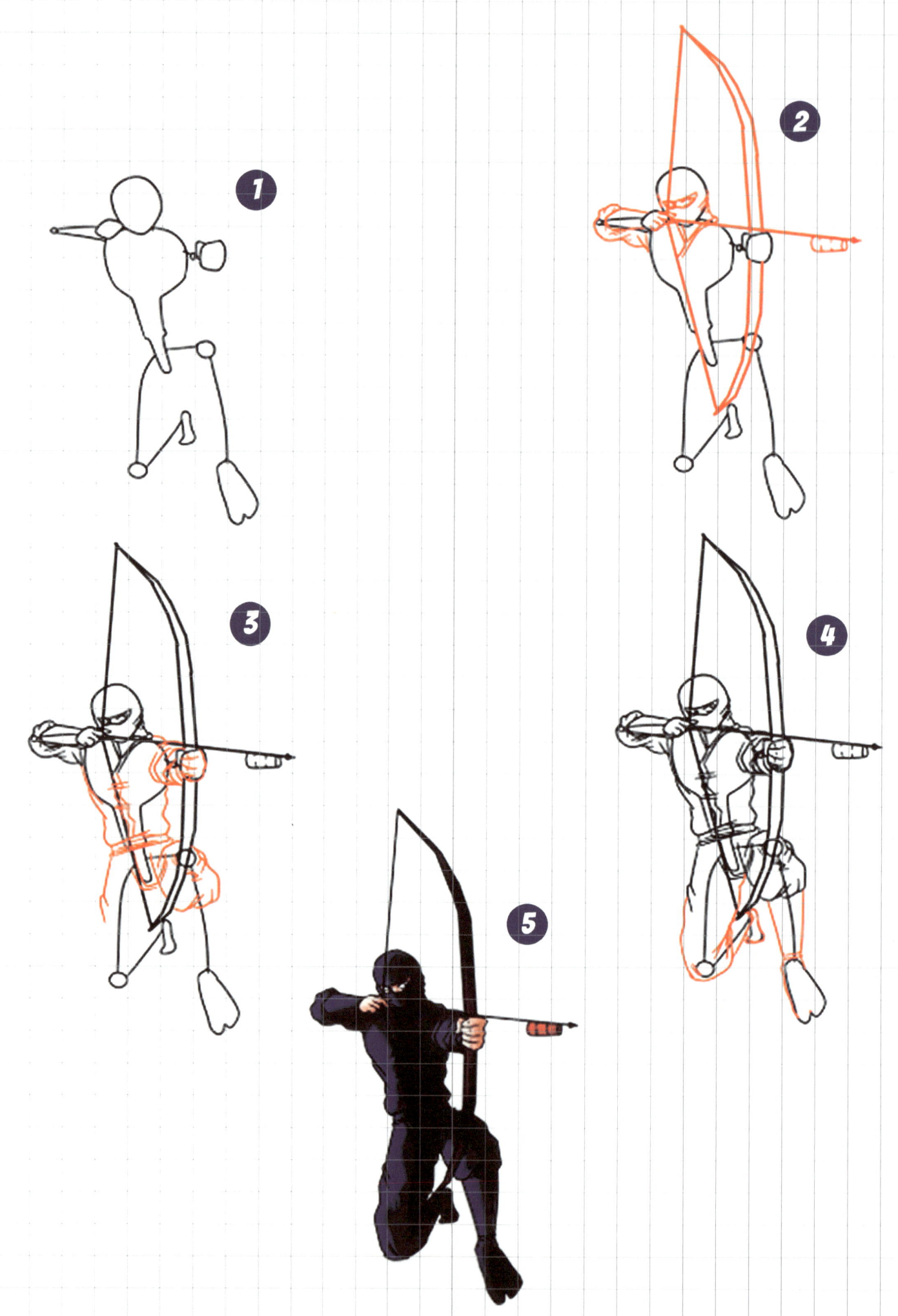

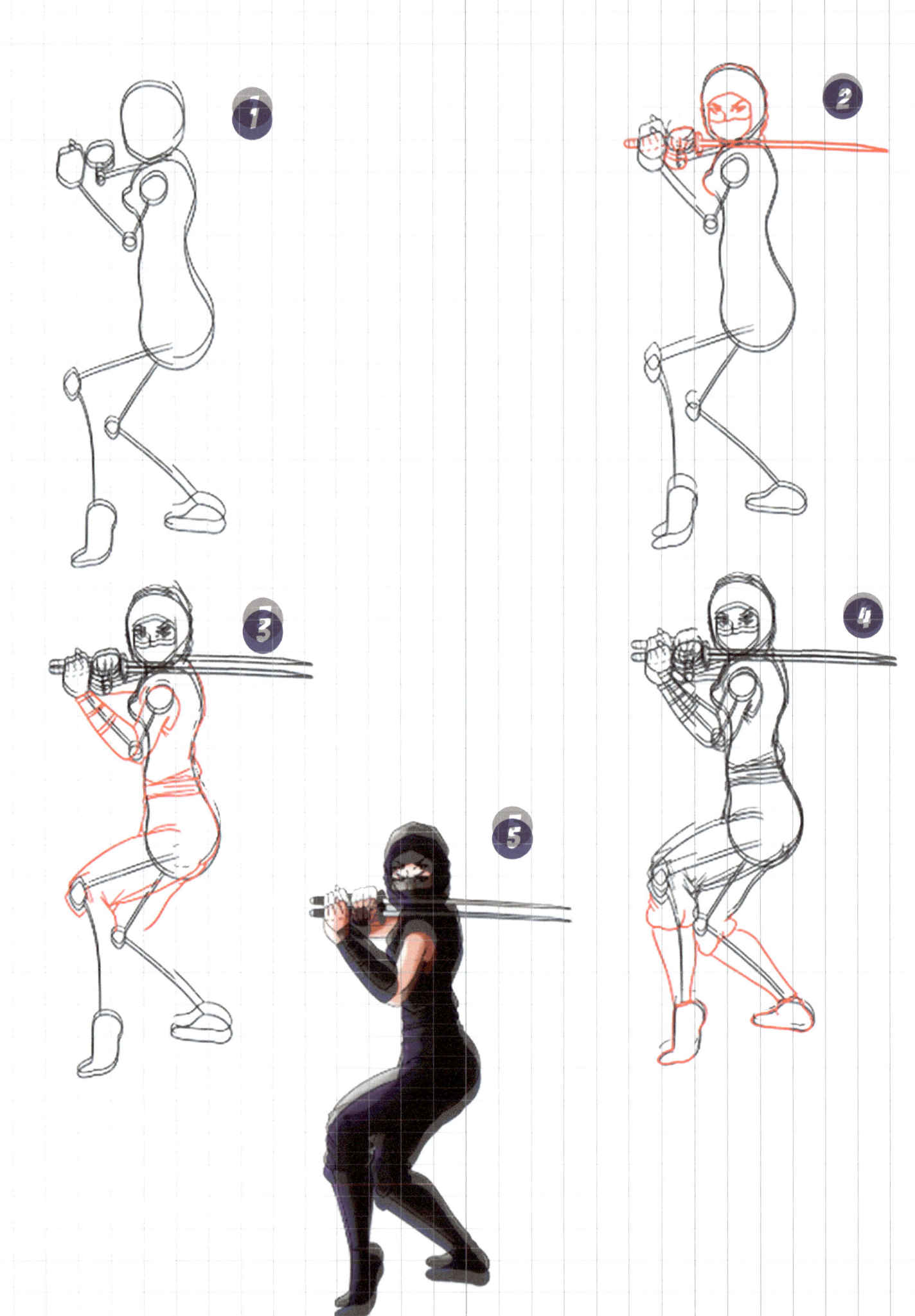

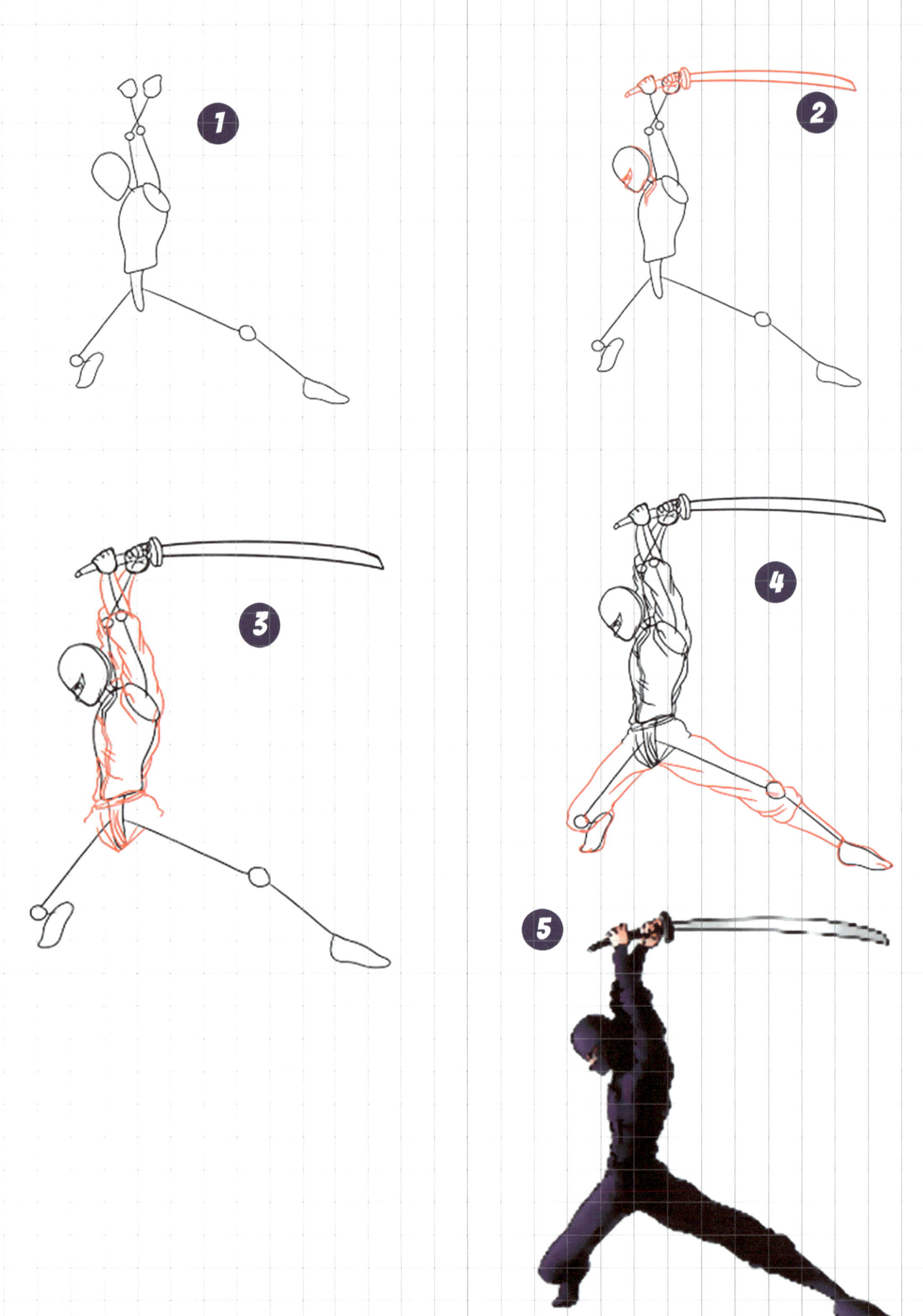

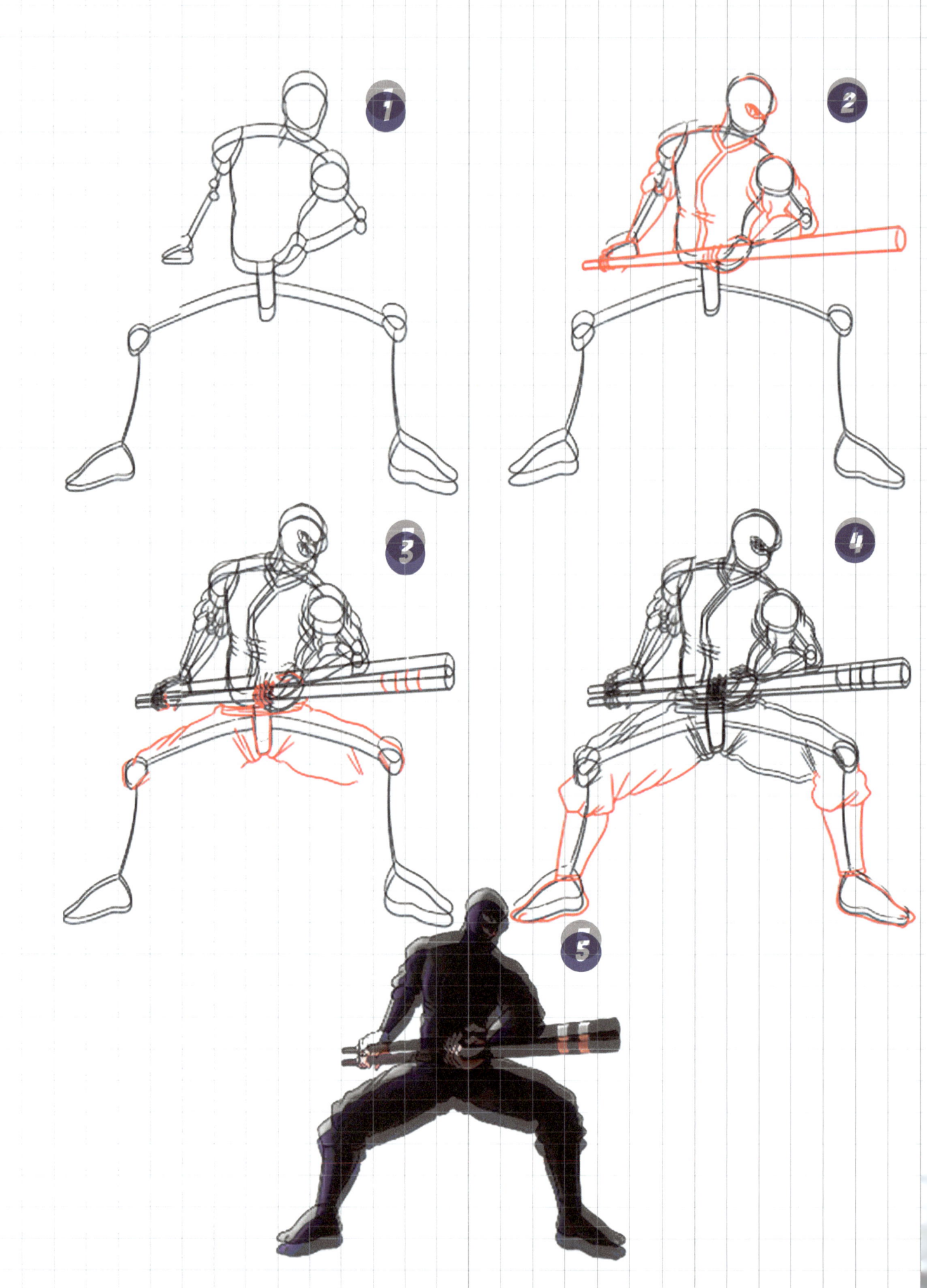

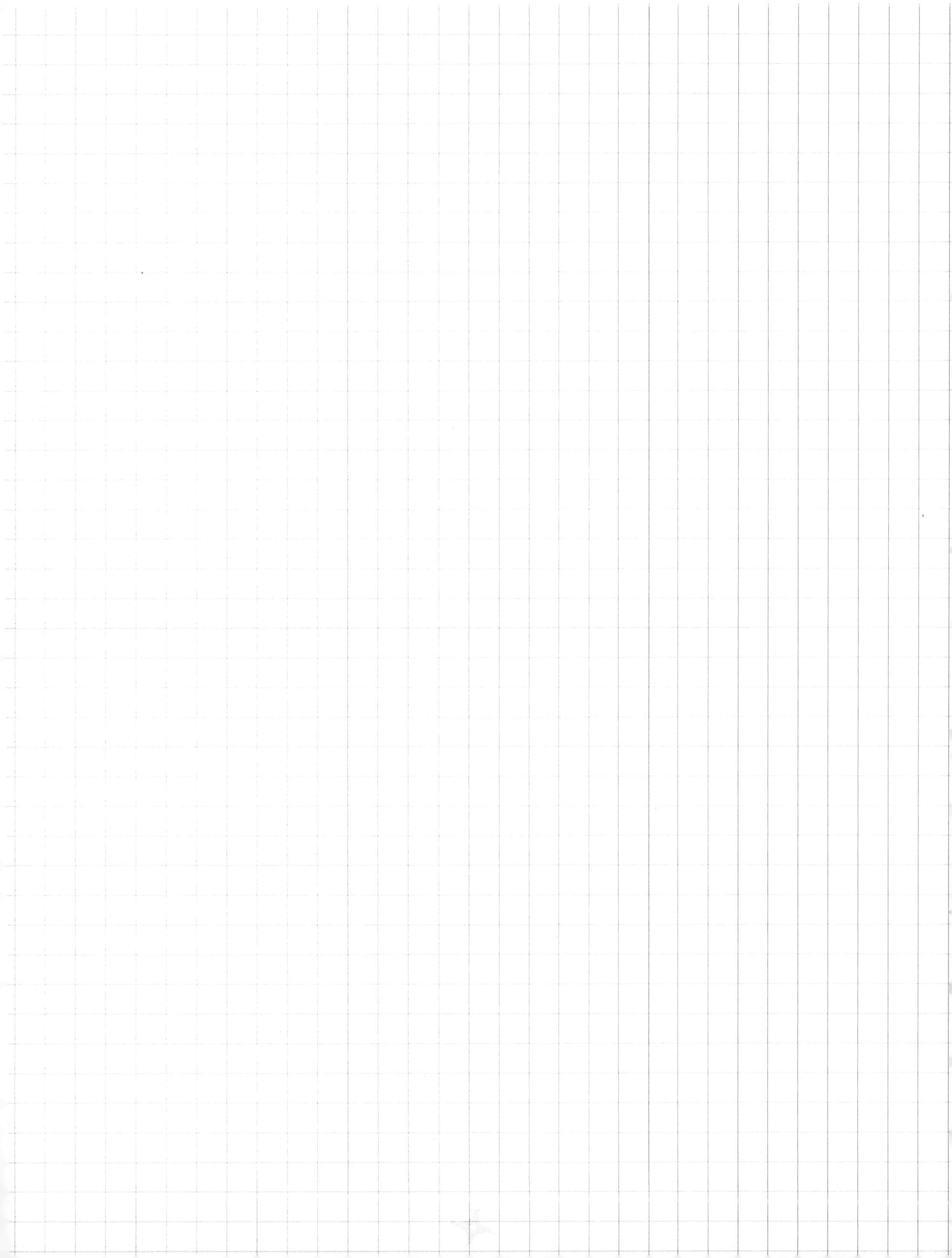

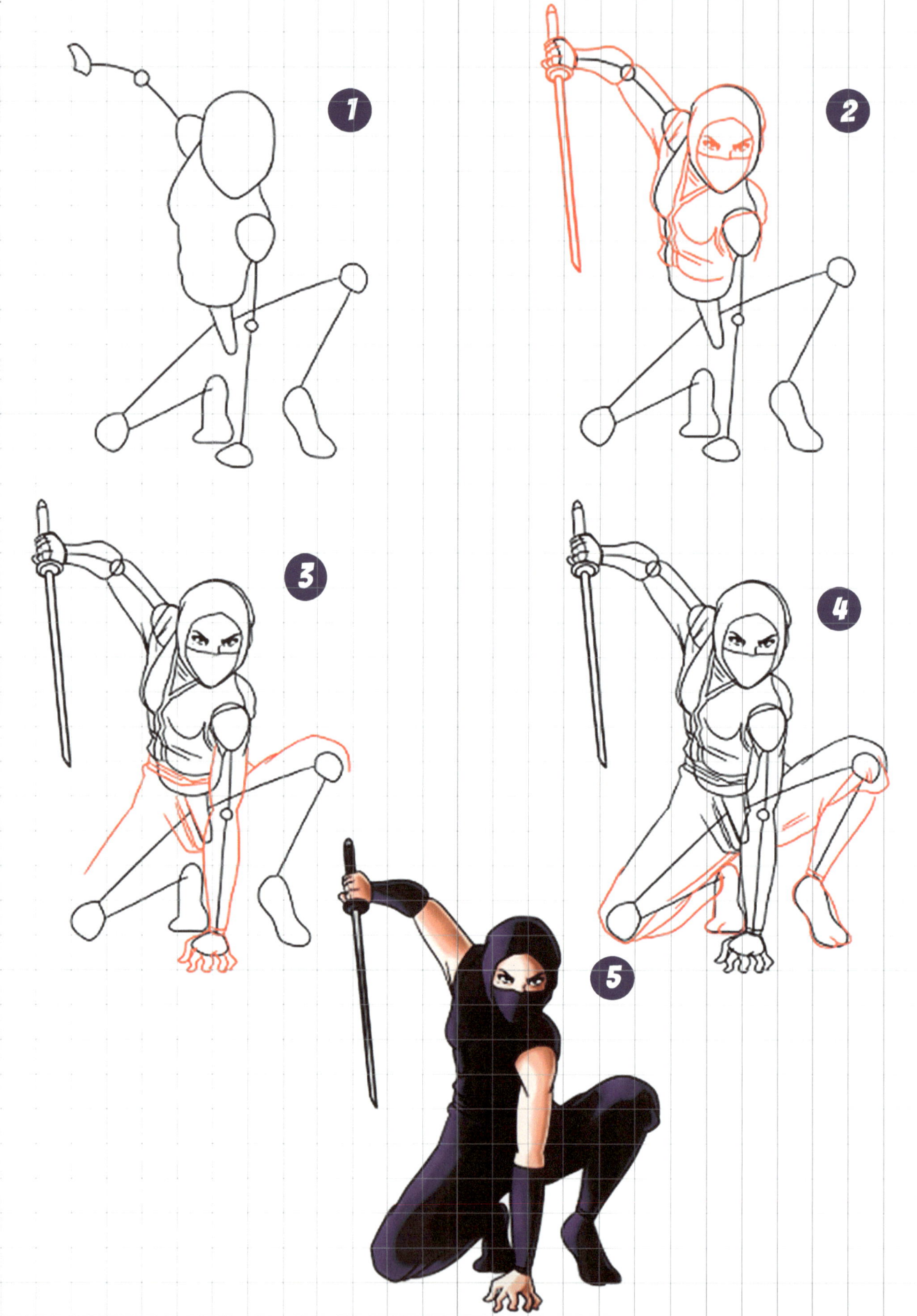

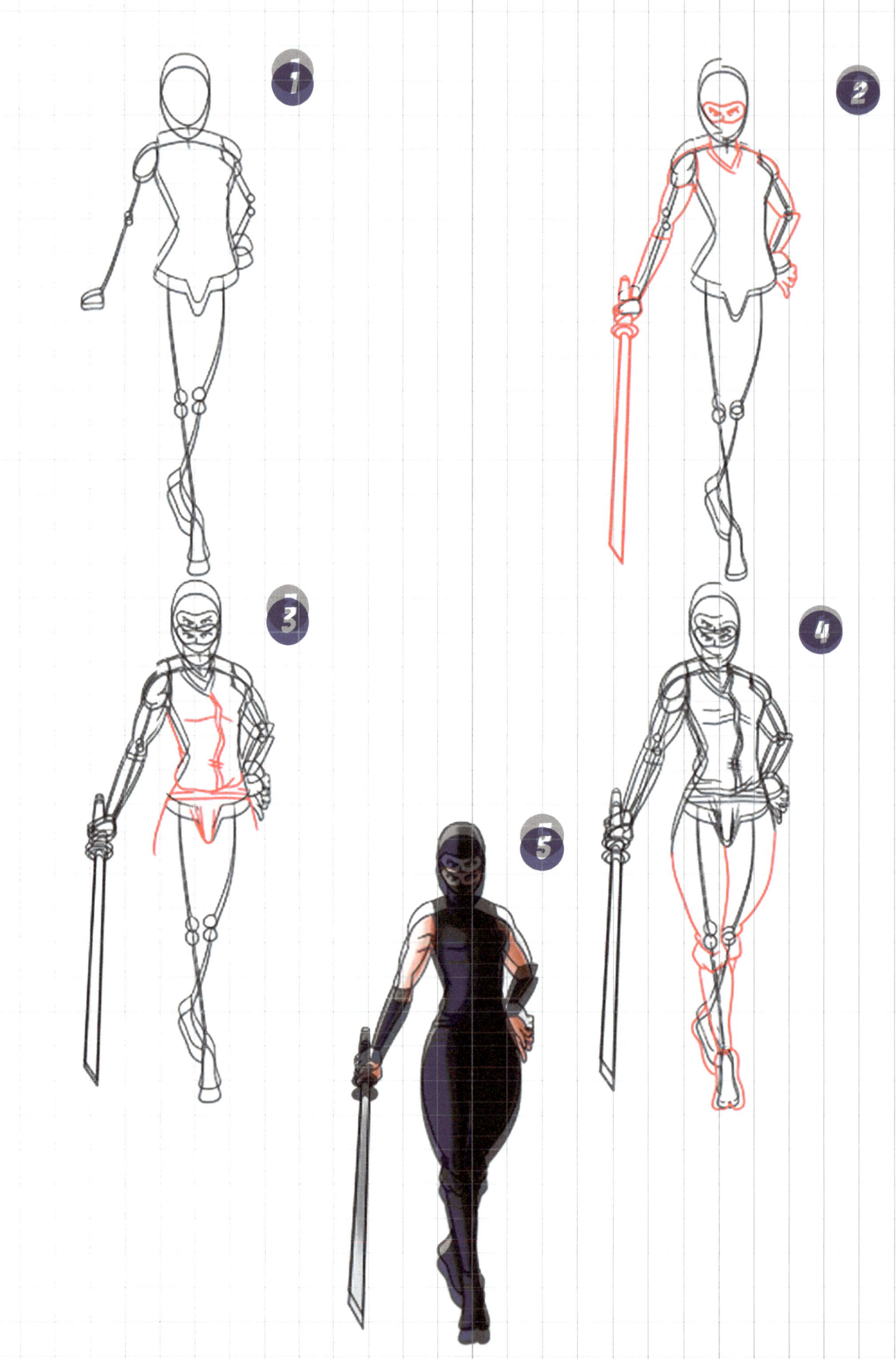

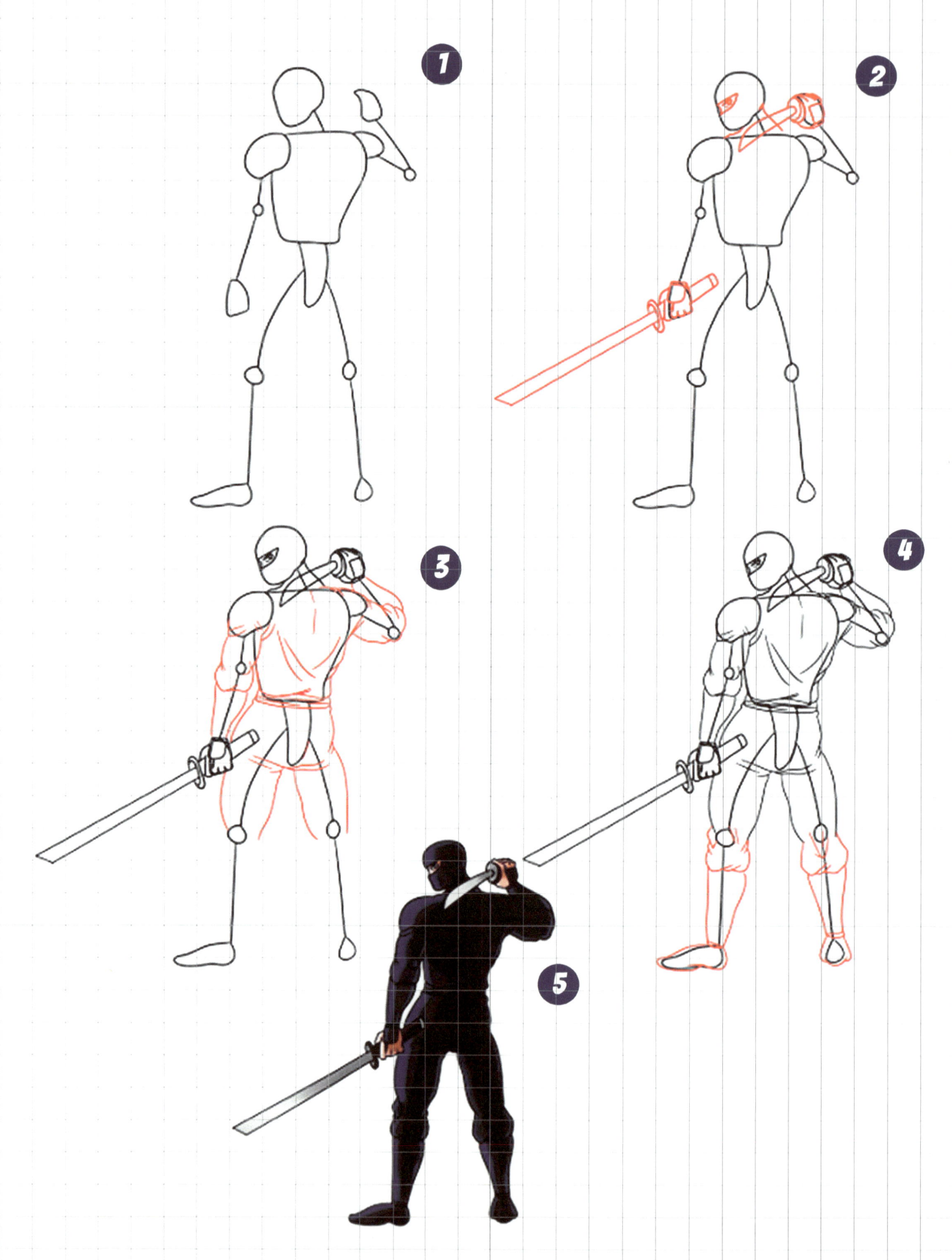

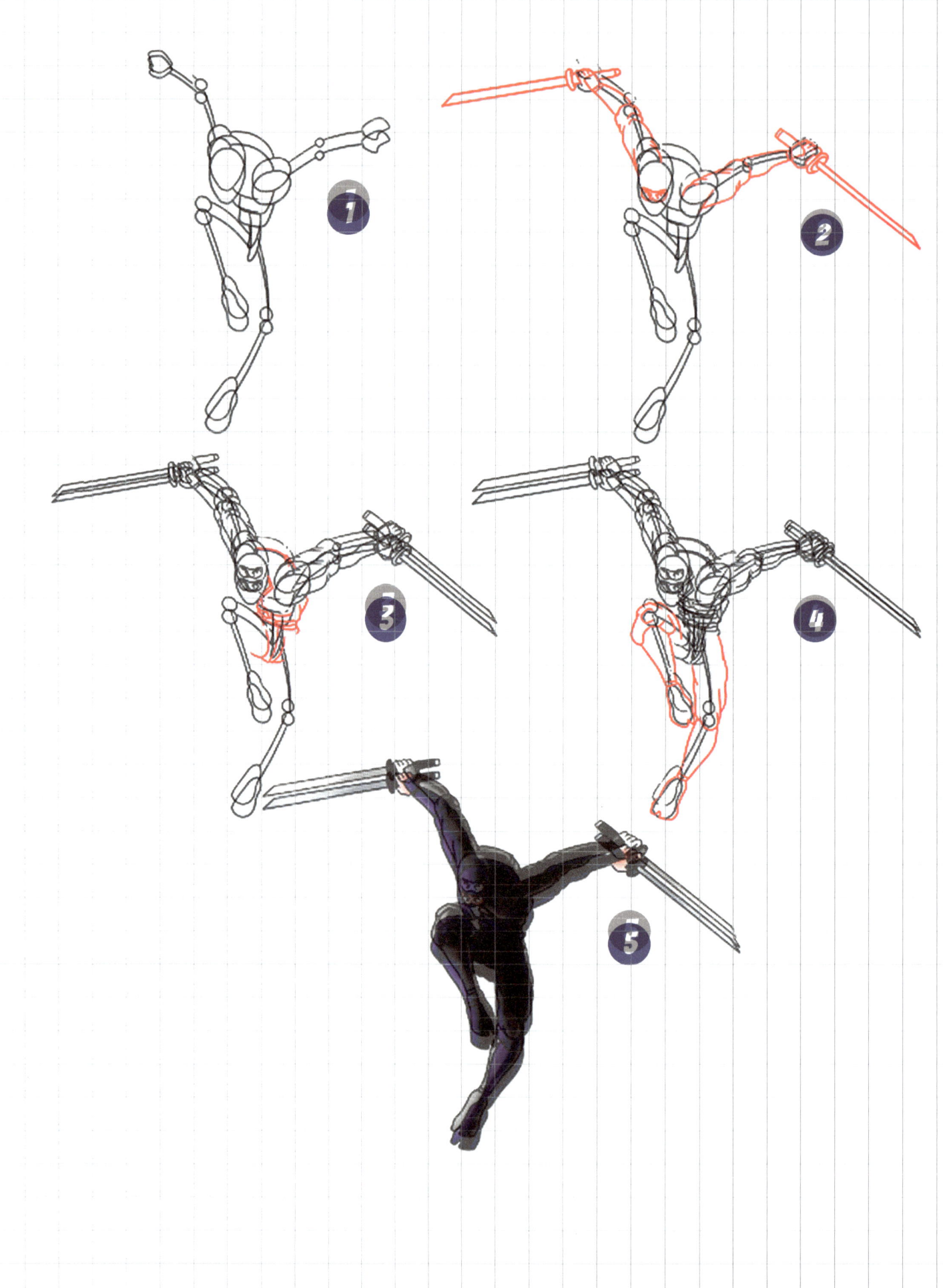

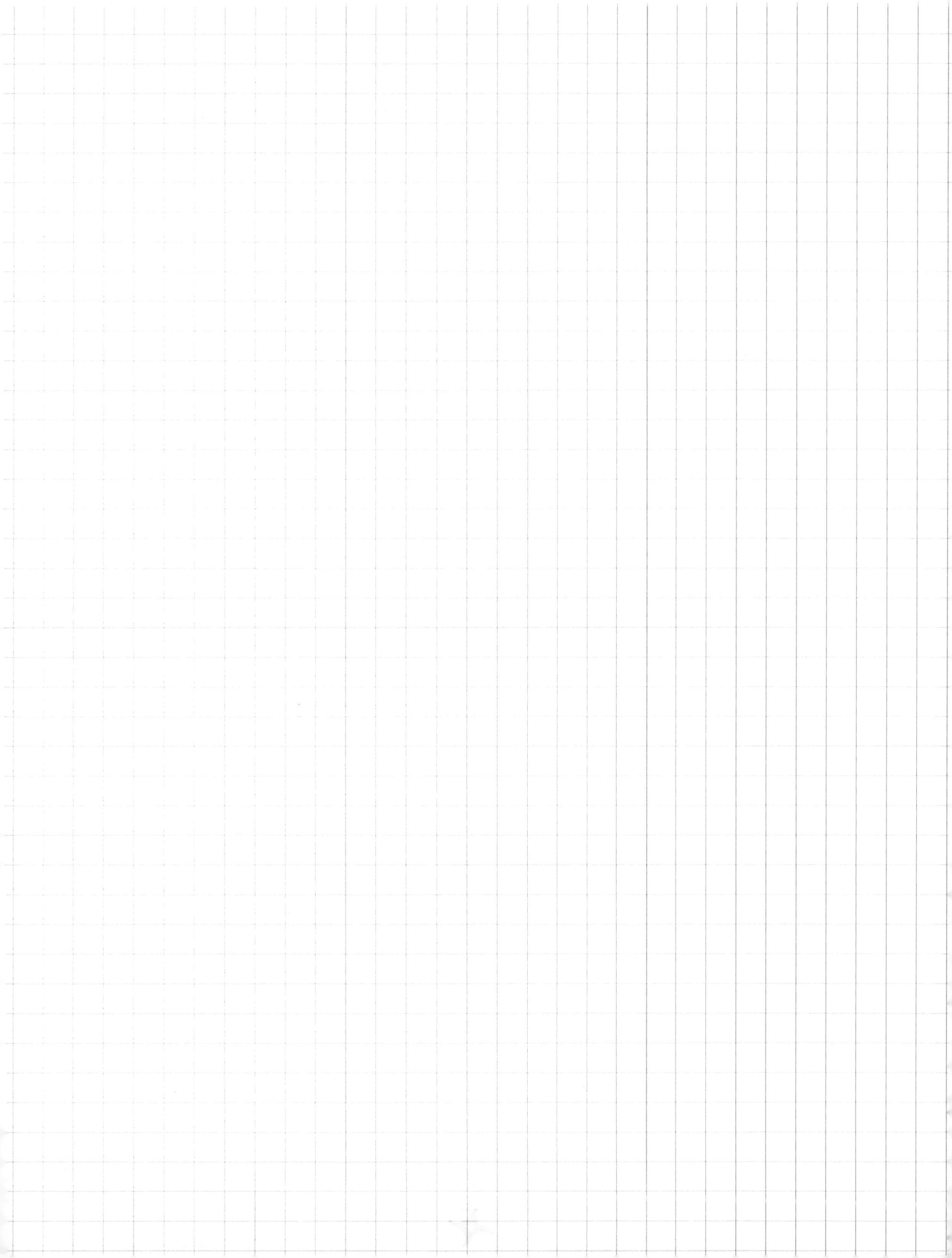

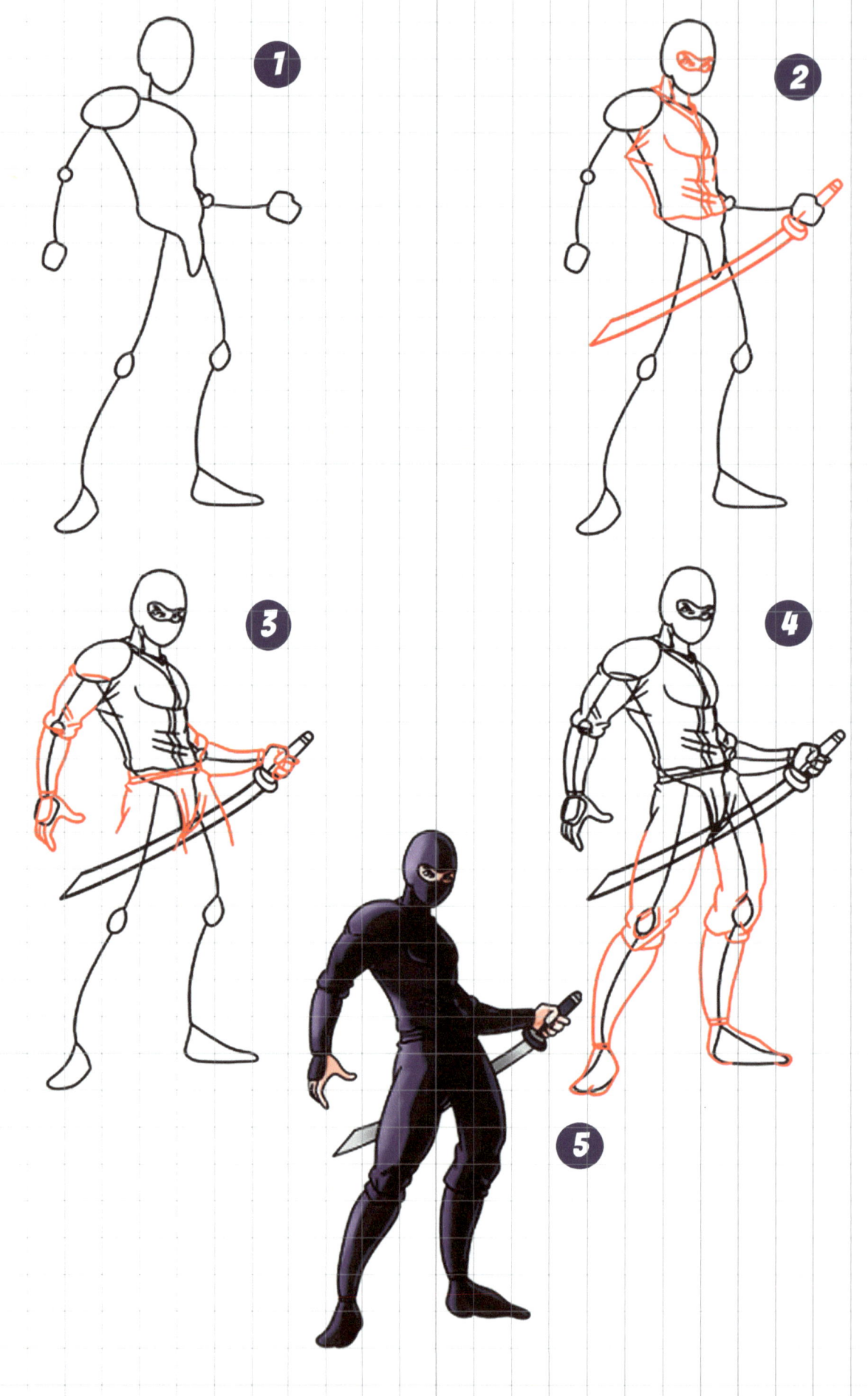

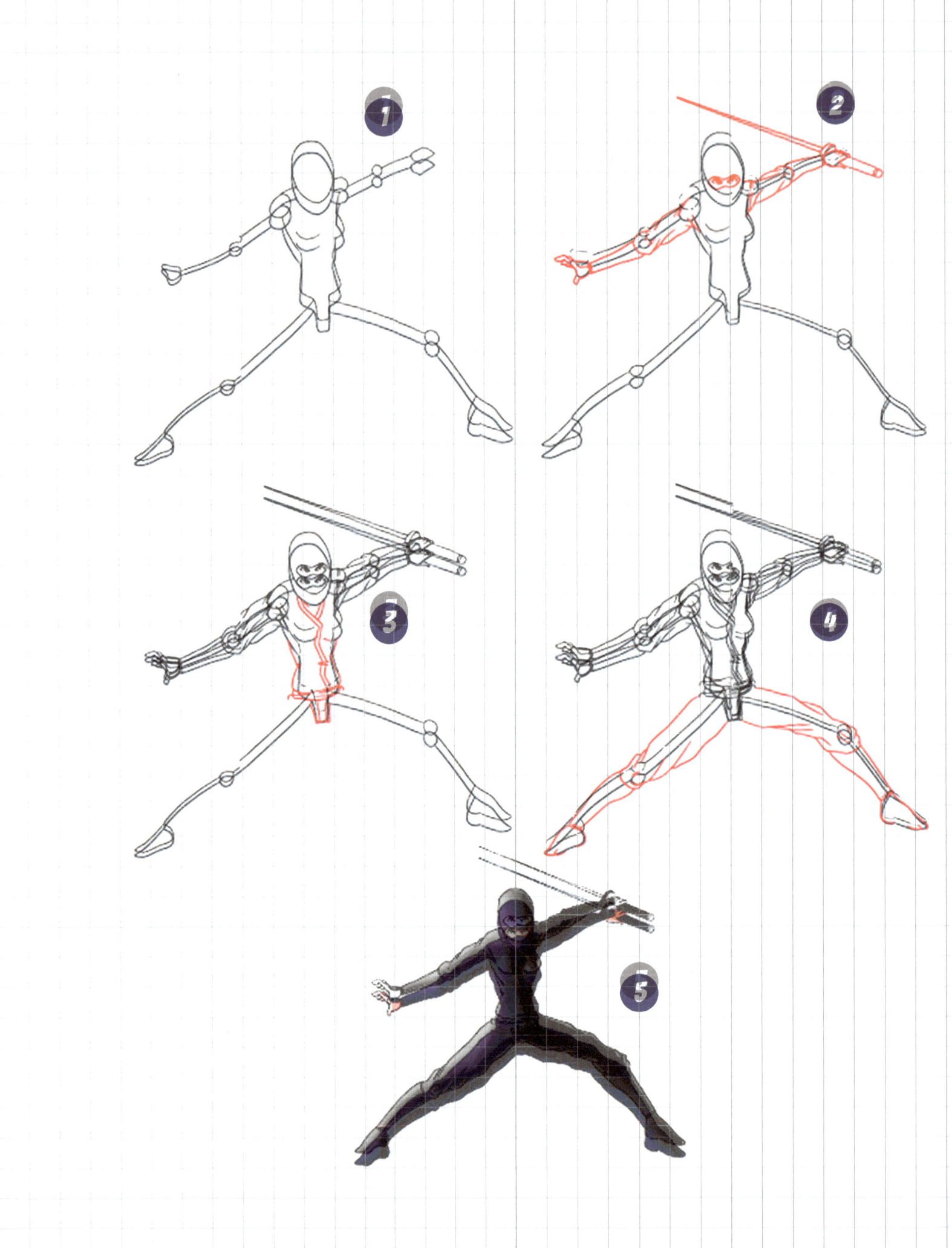

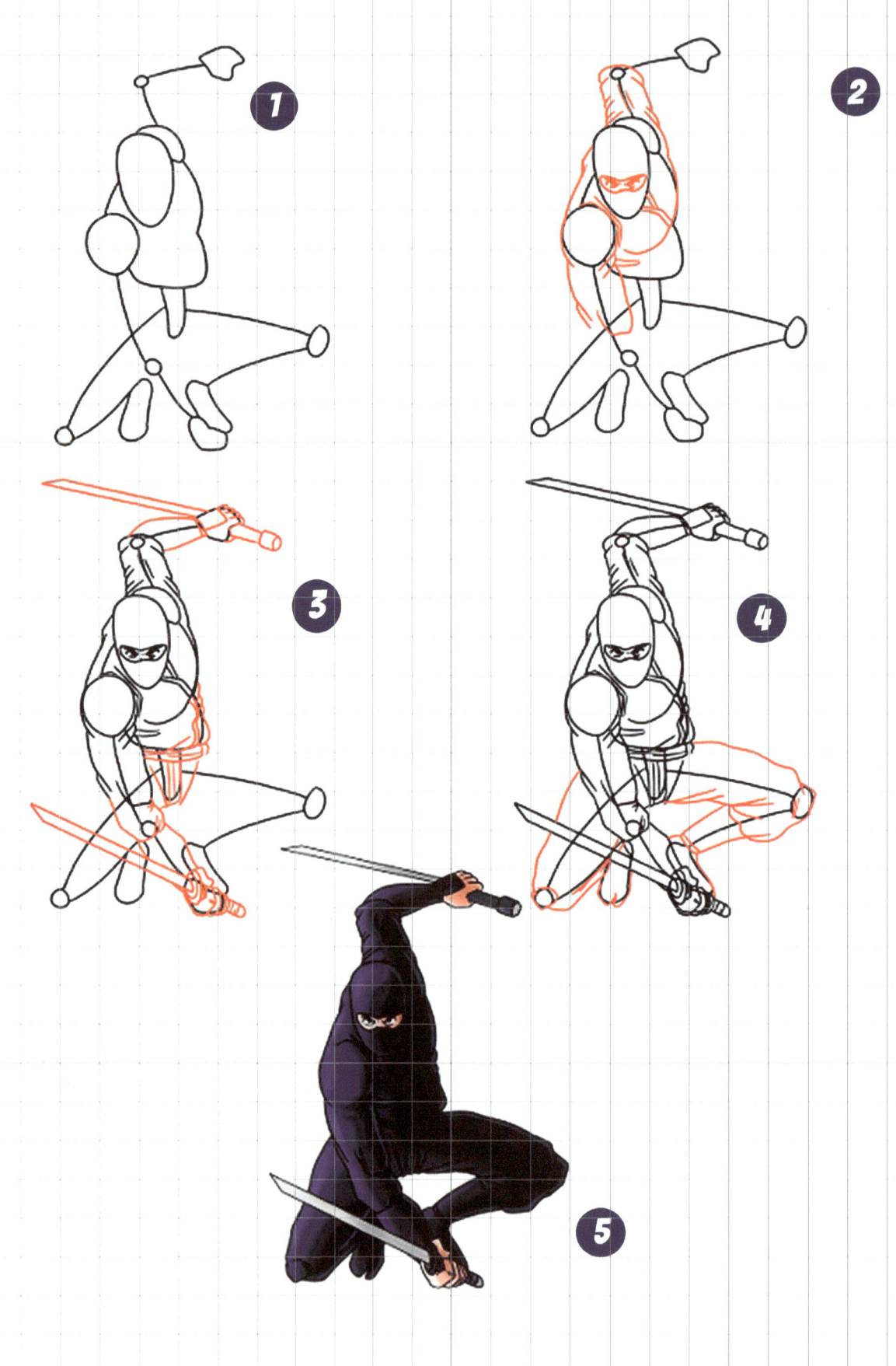

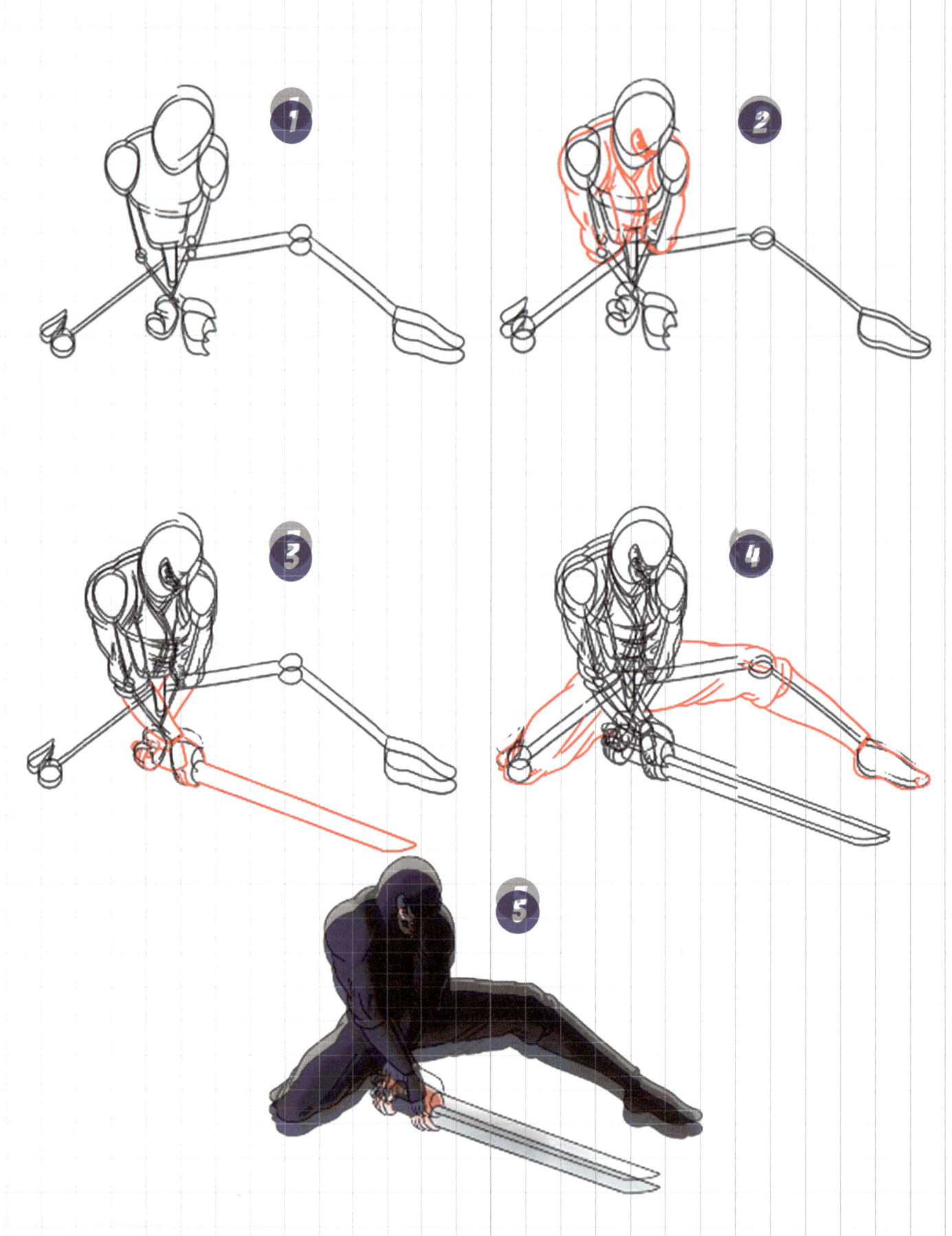

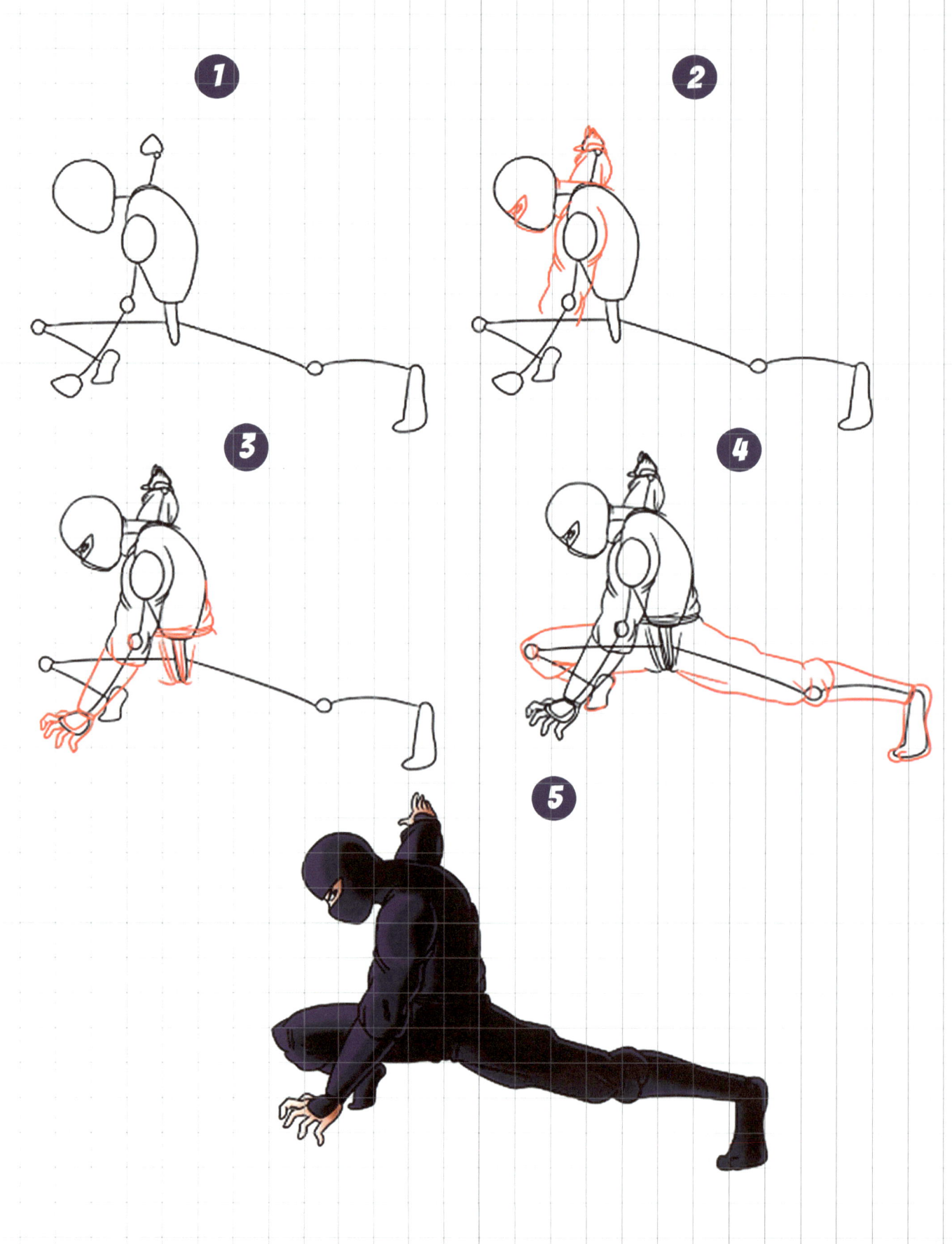

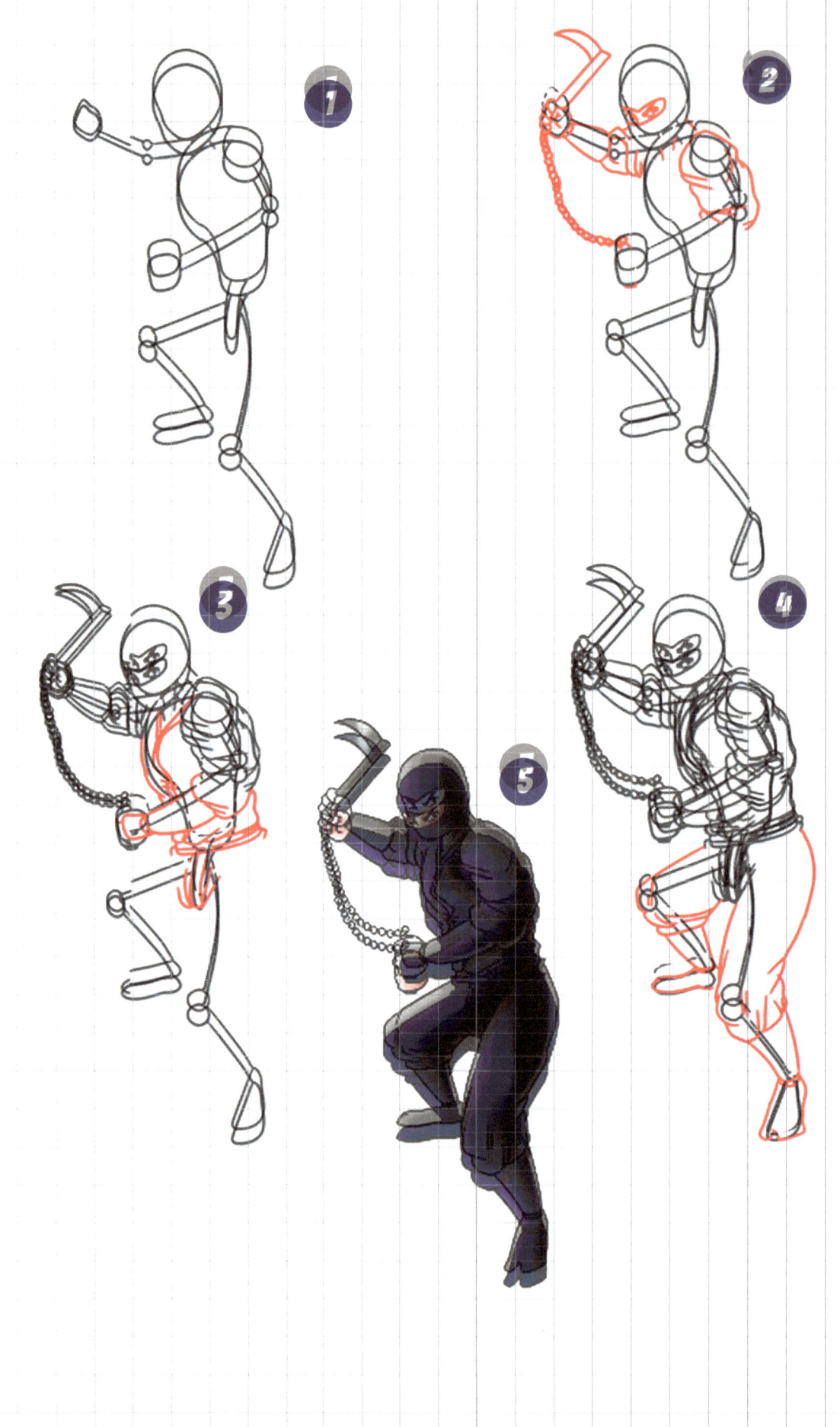

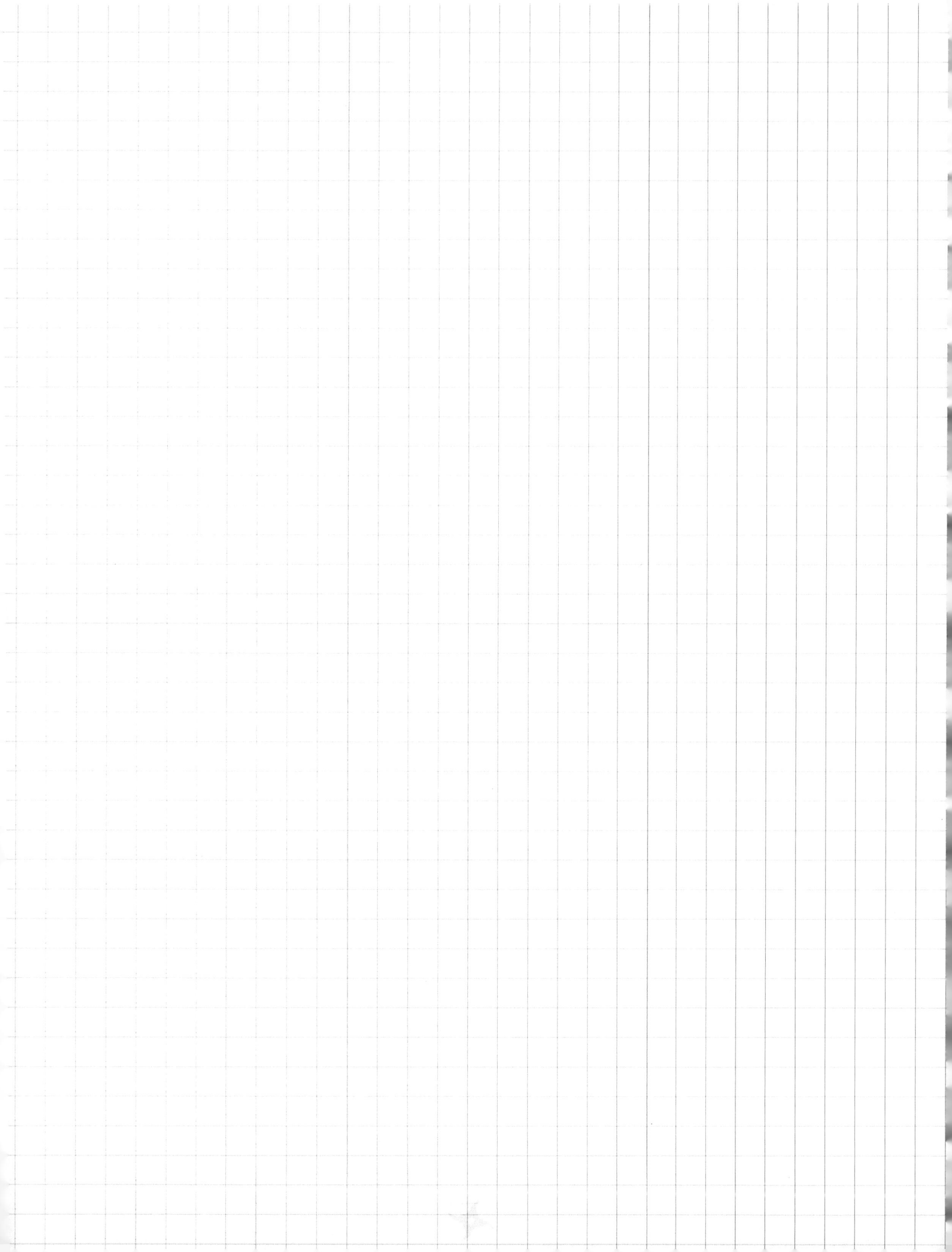

www.ingramcontent.com/pod-product-compliance
Lightning Source LLC
Chambersburg PA
CBHW051919210526
45473CB00006B/2075